MAMAS
DON'T LET
YOUR
BABIES
GROW UP TO BE
A-HOLES

UNFILTERED ADVICE ON
HOW TO RAISE AWESOME KIDS

Karen Alpert
AKA Baby Sideburns

Houghton Mifflin Harcourt
Boston   New York
2021

Dedicated to Zoey and Holden,
who make me feel like I must be doing something right

For information about permission to reproduce selections
from this book, write to trade.permissions@hmhco.com or to
Permissions, Houghton Mifflin Harcourt Publishing Company,
3 Park Avenue, 19th Floor, New York, New York 10016.

hmhbooks.com

Library of Congress Cataloging-in-Publication Data
Names: Alpert, Karen (Blogger), author.
Title: Mamas don't let your babies grow up to be a-holes / Karen Alpert.
Other titles: Mamas don't let your babies grow up to be assholes
Description: New York, New York :
Houghton Mifflin Harcourt Publishing Company, [2021]
Identifiers: LCCN 2020039328 (print) | LCCN 2020039329 (ebook) |
ISBN 9780358346272 (hardback) | ISBN 9780358449799 |
ISBN 9780358449850 | ISBN 9780358346265 (ebook)
Subjects: LCSH: Child rearing. | Parenting. | Socialization.
Classification: LCC HQ769 .A488 2021 (print) | LCC HQ769 (ebook) |
DDC 649/.1 — dc23

Book design by Chrissy Kurpeski
All photographs courtesy of the author

Printed in the United States of America
DOC 10 9 8 7 6 5 4 3 2 1

Contents

Introduction

When babies are born they're basically a-holes, right? They cry and get what they want. They wake you up in the middle of the night and get what they want. They demand food immediately and if they don't get it right away, they just keep screaming until they do. They poop on people. They vomit on people. They pull hair. They grab your boobs without asking. Etc. etc. etc. And even though it's a-hole behavior, it's kind of adorable and acceptable because they're cute little babies.

And then when they turn into toddlers, that stuff starts to get a little annoying. Like when an itty-bitty newborn screams and cries for milk, you're like, "Awwww, are you a thirsty little baby?" But when a toddler wants a cheese stick and they're a messy pile of snot and tears because you didn't walk to the refrigerator fast enough, you're like, "Calm the F down, it's coming." That's right, not as cute.

Now imagine a grownup doing all this stuff. Throwing a tantrum in the middle of the conference room because some intern didn't wheel in the lunch order on time. Or having a complete meltdown because someone cut in line at Bed Bath & Beyond. Or going berserk on an airplane because they're sick and tired of sitting in a cramped seat. Yup, when grownups do stuff like this, we hear about them on the evening news. A-holes, right?

So basically, as parents, we have 18 years to turn our kids into well-adjusted, kind, awesome, rule-abiding human beings by squeezing all the a-holiness out of them. And unfortunately, no one's invented an a-hole juicing machine yet (ewww, they would definitely have to name it something different). So until someone invents that (come onnnn, *Shark Tank*), it's up to us to help our kiddos grow up to be *non* a-holes.

This book shows just a few of the ways I'm attempting to squeeze the a-holiness out of my children before they fly the coop. It seems to be working so far. Usually. Sometimes. Like last Sunday, from 2:47 to 2:53 pm, my kids were well-behaved angels. So I recorded every minute of their angelic behavior and posted it on Instagram and claimed they act like this all the time. Just kidding. But seriously, all kids act like douchenuggets because they're still learning what's okay and what's not. The way I see it, kids who act douchey are douchenuggets, but adults who act douchey are douchebags. Side note: If you're offended by my language, stop reading now. This is not the book for you. Put it down, back away, or feel free to host one of those big bonfire book-burning parties (say that ten times quickly!) and tell all your sensitive friends to buy my book too and you guys can all burn it together. I'll make money, you'll warm your toesies, and we'll all be hunky-dory.

Okay, so have all the prudes left the building? Then hells yeah, let's get down to F'ing business. So WTF was I saying? Oh yeahhh, how do we stop our douchenuggets from growing up to be douchebags? Are you ready for the magic answer? Drum roll please. Badadadadadadada . . . I have no idea. I know what you're thinking. "WHAT?!! I just spent $15 on this book!" ($0 if you were brilliant and checked it out at the library and are willing to hold a book that other people have held while they're pooping.)

But here's the thing. None of us really know WTF we're doing. That mom who rolled her eyes at you because you let your kid wear pajamas in public? She doesn't know what she's doing. That crunchy expert who claims to know how to convince all kids to eat organic raw vegetables covered in flaxseed? She doesn't know what she's doing. That mom who lives across the street in that giant McMansion whose perfectly-coiffed kiddos are always wearing matchy-matchy Lilly Pulitzer dresses? She doesn't know what she's doing. I mean, they all act like they know what they're doing, but I guarantee there's been a time or two that they've all broken down in tears and curled up at the bottom of their closet in the fetal position around a bottle of vodka or a chocolate candy bar or a flaxseed vegan nut wafer (I just made that up). But seriously, NONE of us REALLY know WTF we're doing because there's no magic answer or instruction manual when it comes to parenting. And kids are like snowflakes — every one is different. Of course, kids these days are like snowflakes in other ways too, but I'll get to that later. So anyways (yes, I purposely use fake words sometimes because it helps my mistakes blend in like I did them on purpose), if I don't know all the magic answers, who am I to write a book about it?

I'm just your average mom.

I'm the mom who yells too much when my kids won't get their shoes on. I'm the mom who forgets to order the birthday cake until the day of the party. I'm the mom who has a stack of Girl Scout patches in the junk drawer because I'm too lazy to attach them to my daughter's vest. But guess what I've realized? That's not the shit that makes you a good parent. Being a good parent is all about one thing: raising your kids to be kind, happy, self-sufficient human beings. I know, barf me out the door, it sounds so hokey and lame, but it's true. And I think my parenting philosophies are working. Kinda. Sorta. Well, except for on the days they're not working and my kids are acting like jerkwads and I second-guess everything I'm doing. But on the whole, my kids seem to be getting less and less douchey every year. It could be dumb luck, but mayyyybe the things I'm doing are turning them into decent humans.

Like how I taught both of my kids how to use a washing machine before they were tall enough to reach the buttons. And how I let them wear pretty much anything they want as long as they're not gonna freeze, burn, or look like an exhibitionist. And how I actually want them to *lose* some of their soccer games. And how I teach them to be extra nice to bullies. And how the same way I schedule "after-school" activities, I also schedule "nothing-to-do" time. Oh crap, I just told you this whole book in one paragraph. Okay, well, that was the synopsis, but maybe you want a little more explanation, so if you do, keep reading. If you don't, hopefully you've already walked out of the bookstore and lost your receipt and can't return this book now.

Bottom line, this isn't your average parenting advice book that's preachy or scientific or gonna tell you what to do. I didn't go to psychology school or get a master's in anything. The only letters I have after my name are M.O.M. But I have something much more important that proves I can write a parenting book. A nine-year-old daughter who's a picky eater and ridiculously dramatic but who's turning out to be pretty damn awesome, and a seven-year-old son who eats with his mouth open and can burp the alphabet, but who's also sensitive, caring, and hard-working. I mean, maybe they'll both grow up to be drug-dealing serial killers (if they do, come ask me for a refund), but I don't think so.

And honestly, feel free to ignore parts/most/all of this book if you don't agree with what I'm saying. I don't give a shit. I'm just a regular mom sitting here in my fat pants on the couch typing this (total lie, I'm actually sitting in my yoga pants outside of the Apple store while they're fixing my iPhone but that sounds way too cliché so I changed it), and some of what I say might be good for you and your family, but some of it might not be. I'm NOT here to give you advice. I'm just here to tell you how *I* handle stuff and maybe it'll help you or maybe it won't. I'm basically the opposite of that lady who rolls her eyes at you because you wore pajama pants to school drop-off because you didn't have time to get dressed. Or pajama pants to school pickup because you inhaled a whole bag of Doritos and now they're the only things that fit.

But no matter what you wear to school — pajamas, Lululemon, Gucci, spit-up, no bra, the shirt you wore yesterday — aren't we all just trying to do the same thing? Trying not to F up our kids too much, putting a little aside for therapy just in case, and hopefully turning our kids into decent human beings, aka NOT a-holes.

———∘———

CHAPTER 1

You Are Not Your Kiddo's Servant

OKAY, SO IMAGINE THIS. You get to live somewhere for free, and the fridge is always stocked with awesome shit, and there's a pantry full of your favorite snacks that magically reappear every week, and the utility bills are all paid for, and someone does the dishes and washes your clothes and will even wash your favorite t-shirt quickly if it's in your hamper and you want to wear it that very day. In fact, you can get someone to wipe your butt for you if you ask really nicely — or if you scream at the top of your lungs for long enough. This is what it's like when you're a kid.

And then imagine this. One day someone gently wakes you up in the morning and says they have some exciting news. "Surprise, you're a grownup now! Get the F out of this house and go take care of yourself!!" And you're like, "Wha-WHAT?!! But wait, what is this big white box that has buttons on it that say hot, warm, cold, and delicates? And why isn't anyone pouring me my Sugary Boogery O's for breakfast? And who's gonna wipe my tushie? Mom? Mom?! MOMMMMM?!!!" And everyone in the dorm is like, "STFU and wipe your own butt." Because your mommy isn't there anymore. And unfortunately, she didn't teach you jack when you were living with her, so basically now you're screwed.

The way I see it, parents have 18 years to teach their kids how to take care of themselves or they'll come back home and crash in their basement for the rest of their lives. Although I always wonder why adults who move back home always live in the basement. Hellllooo, why wouldn't you just move into your old room? Oh, is it because you want a little more privacy? Tough. You move back in, you're sleeping in a twin bed loaded with stuffed animals and *Paw Patrol* sheets.

HOLDEN: Mom, can I have some milk?
ME:
HOLDEN: Mom, can I PLEASE have some milk?
ME:
HOLDEN: Mom, MAY I please have some milk?
ME:
HOLDEN: Ugggh, what am I doing wrong?
ME: You're not getting up and walking to the fridge to get some milk.

FIFTY BASIC THINGS TO TEACH YOUR KIDS BEFORE THEY FLY THE COOP

Here's the bad news. This list is gonna seem daunting. Here's the good news. You literally have 18 years to complete it. Like you can just do three of these things a year and you'll still get it all done earlier than you need to. And really, all you have to do to complete it is keep going about life the way you always do but make sure your kiddos put their iPads down once in a while and watch you so they'll learn it all by osmosis. So here goes. Fifty basic things to teach your douchenuggets so they won't turn into incompetent adults:

1. How to make pasta
2. How to rinse out the sink before the toothpaste hardens
3. How to hang a picture straight
4. How to hang a group of pictures so it doesn't matter if they're perfectly straight
5. How a credit card works and what happens if you don't pay it off on time
6. How to ask for a raise when you deserve it. And how to know when you don't deserve it yet.
7. How to apologize when you're wrong
8. How to apologize when you were NOT wrong but it's not worth dragging out the fight
9. How to flip the couch cushions occasionally
10. How to save money for a rainy day

11. How to save money for something you really want
12. How to put up a curtain rod so you don't have to crouch down every time you're naked and walking past your windows
13. How to replace the toilet paper when it runs out
14. How to unwrap the package of toilet paper before you put it under the sink
15. How to clean the shower, the sink, the toilet, the countertop, the stove, the oven, the microwave, the floors, the ceilings, and everything in between
16. How to shovel the snow before it turns into ice
17. How to spackle and fix a nail hole in the wall
18. How to clean up a spill before it gets worse
19. How to repeat someone's name when you meet them so you're more likely to remember it
20. How to politely ask someone's name again if you forget it
21. How to turn off the lights when you leave a room
22. How to write a thank-you note
23. How to clean up when houseguests are coming over
24. How to *straighten* up when friends are coming over
25. How to make grilled cheese in the pan, not just the toaster
26. How to tip waiters, bartenders, hairdressers, bellhops, skycaps, shuttle drivers, the pizza delivery guy, housekeepers, movers, and anyone else who basically makes a living off people's generosity
27. How to do the laundry
28. How to put in an entire load of laundry even when you only have one thing you want to wash
29. How to recycle

30. How to vote
31. How to shut your mouth and not complain if you didn't vote
32. How to volunteer
33. How to send your food back nicely in a restaurant if it didn't come out right
34. How to make a cup of coffee so you don't have to put on clothes, walk to the store, and shell out three bucks every time you need some caffeine
35. How to exercise even when you don't feel like it
36. How to be extra generous around the holidays, especially to the people who make a difference in your life every day
37. How to go to the doctor when you're sick
38. How to go to the doctor, the dermatologist, the dentist, and the gyno when you're NOT sick
39. How to check the oil in your car and put more air in the tires and change a flat tire so you don't have to accept help from some sketchy dude on the side of the highway and end up in the bottom of a pit putting the lotion in the basket
40. How to pick out good produce at the grocery store (except for cantaloupes because I'm 47 and I still have no idea how to pick out a good cantaloupe)
41. How not to yap on your cell phone like an a-hole in public
42. How to glance behind you when you go through a door and hold it open if someone else is there
43. How to stand aside when the elevator doors open in case someone is getting out
44. How to ask "Which floor?" when you're the one standing next to the buttons on the elevator

45. How to be patient and kind at annoying places like the DMV
46. How to move over when someone is walking straight toward you on the sidewalk
47. How to smile when you walk past someone and not just look at the ground
48. How to win nicely
49. How to lose nicely
50. How to change a light bulb so you don't call the electrician and get charged $100 for a $2 fix

- - - - - - - - -

ME: Hey, buddy, did you change your underwear?
HOLDEN: Yes.
ME: Then how come they're the same Star Wars ones you wore to bed?
HOLDEN: I have two like that.
ME: No you don't.
HOLDEN: I bought new ones.
ME: That fast?
HOLDEN: Amazon Prime.

- - - - - - - - -

Whenever I tell Zoey she has to do her chores before she goes out to play, I feel like Cinderella's bitchy stepmother. But then I remember something. Cinderella turned out to be a totally kick-ass woman, so maybe her stepmom actually knew WTF she was doing.

- - - - - - - - -

HOLDEN: Mom, I just realized something.
ME: What?
HOLDEN: Dogs can lick their penises but people can't.
ME: Yup.
HOLDEN: Why can't they?
ME: Because nothing would ever get done if they could.

- - - - - - - - -

THE TIME I THOUGHT GETTING MY KIDS PETS WOULD TEACH THEM ABOUT RESPONSIBILITY. BWAHAHAHAHAHAHA, I'M SUCH AN IDIOT.

Holy crap. WHAT just happened? No, seriously, was I abducted by aliens or something because someone just took over my brain and made me say yes and now it's only 30 minutes later and I'm like WTF did I do? I am regretting my decision BIG TIME. You know how when you go to Target and you end up buying all these impulse items you didn't plan on buying, like a new hair dryer and tiki torches and an ottoman? Annoying, right? Ennnnnnh, that's nothing. You know where it REALLY sucks to buy impulse items? Let me tell you.

It all started one day when the kids and I were driving home.

ME: Hey, guys, we just need to stop and pick up some kitty litter.

Note, I did not say let's just pick up some kitty litter and a whole F'ing zoo, but for some reason that's what my douchenuggets heard. We walk into PetSmart and before the automatic doors even close behind us . . .

KIDS: Pleeeeease can we get something?
ME: No.
THEM: Can we just get a bird?
ME: No.
THEM: I want a hamster!! Pleeeeeeease can I?
ME: NO.
THEM: But we don't have a pet!!
ME: What are you talking about? You have a pet. A cat.
ZOEY: That's YOUR pet.
HOLDEN: Yeah, we want our OWN pets.
TOGETHER: Please please pleeeeeease, can we pleeeease just get a fish?
ME: A fish?

Shit shit shit, I already broke the cardinal rule. I showed the itty-bittiest sign of caving and now they are allllll over me like white on rice.

THEM: Pleeeease, we'll take care of it completely, we swear!!! We'll do everything!

FYI, if your kid says this, DO NOT BELIEVE THEM. They are pathological liars and there's no such thing as a child who takes care of their own pet without you constantly nagging them. Of course at the time I didn't know this yet and I was like, perfect, this will be an awesome way to teach them about responsibility. And besides, how bad can a fish be?

ME: Hmmm, one fish, guys?
ZOEY: One for him and one for me.
ME: In *one* tank?
ZOEY: Yessss!!!

And before I even answer them, they're running around the store like maniacs because I said yes even though I haven't really.

So we track down the PetSmart guy, let's just call him Angus (yes this is a fake name just in case I ever go back to kill him, and yes I picked it on purpose because if you remove one letter, that's what this guy is as far as I'm concerned), and we tell him what we want. Two fish.

ME: Two small, easy-to-care-for fish, preferably the kind
that have a really short lifespan.

(Like an hour or two)

ANGUS: A fish? You don't want fish.

I shit you not, the pet store guy, as in the guy who's supposed to convince naïve humans to buy animals, tells me we don't want fish. All of a sudden I'm loving Angus.

ANGUS: Fish are super hard to care for. You want a gecko.

WTF Angus?

ME: Ummmm, no. We do NOT want a gecko.
ANGUS: Geckos are way easier than fish. I have nine
geckos in my house.

And he proceeds to tell me allllllll about his nine geckos, only I'm not really listening because he's talking about lizards that just cost money and don't cuddle so as far as I'm concerned there is ZERO reason to buy one, and I'm picturing his dark apartment full of nine glowing aquariums with geckos and there's only one thing that's going through my head. Seeeerial killlllller.

But apparently Angus isn't a serial killer and actually knows WTF he's doing because pretty soon I realize the only way to get Angus to shut up about his nine geckos is to agree to buy one. Good strategy, Anus, uhhh, I mean Angus.

And then it gets worse. Zoey says she doesn't want a gecko but wants her *own* pet and she's chosen a guinea pig, and I must be high or something because I say yes, but only after I've committed to buying her one does Angus explain to us that you can't just have *one* guinea pig because guinea pigs are herd animals and need companions or else they get really mean and start eating people's eyes out. "Don't worry," he tells us, "having two guinea pigs is pretty much the same thing as having one." Except now I know that's a total lie because guinea pigs must have ten butts or something because they constantly poop, so if you get *two* guinea pigs, basically you're buying twenty butts that poop. So yes, TWO guinea pigs does matter, Anus.

So we head to the register with a cartful of impulse items — a gecko, two guinea pigs, and a SHITLOAD of supplies.

CASHIER: That'll be $242984823589. Oh, and would you like to make a donation today to the *You Don't Want Sweet Little Innocent Dogs to Die* Shelter?

Hmm, at this moment, I kinda do want all animals to die. But I can't say that out loud.

ME: Fine, add a dollar to our total.

And the kids walk out of the store with their new pets AND something else. Two GINORMOUS smiles and a crapload of new responsibilities. And that's when I realize something. Wow, even though this is going to be a ton of work and money, maybe it's worth it.

Two days later: No it's not.

ME: Have you washed your hands?
ZOEY: Yes.
ME: Really? That seemed too fast.
ZOEY: Oh, I thought you meant ever.

Holy crap, I just drove by my neighbor's house and you're not going to believe this, but their eleven-year-old daughter was out there mowing the lawn. Yup, they made their eleven-year-old girl push around that big heavy lawnmower!! All I could think was, OMG, I can't wait until Zoey is eleven so I can do that.

THE PICTURE ZOEY DREW FOR ME THAT I WILL NEVER EVER FRAME

Oh no, she didn't. Oh yes, she did. I mean, I know kids do stupid stuff all the time and they don't even realize it, but when Zoey did this I was like nuh-uhhhh, that is not okay. Not okay at all.

It all started on the first snow day of the year when I dragged my ass out of bed and managed to scrounge up all of the kids' snow gear, which is NEVER an easy task. I mean, I'm not one of those moms who has a shitload of snow gloves and neck warmers and thermals lying around. I'm the cheap mom who buys one of each item at Costco and then screams at her kids when they accidentally leave something at school.

As soon as the kids were dressed in their thermal underwear and snow pants, they bolted outside to play with all their friends. And then the entire neighborhood came to my house afterward to have hot cocoa because I stupidly said, "The more the merrier," even though that's total bullshit and the second they all came into my house, I was thinking, "Agghhh, why did I decide to have 20 kids at my house and agree to feed them liquid chocolate that hypes them up and stains everything?!!"

Speaking of chocolate, Zoey spilled a crapload down the

front of her thermals, but she kept wearing them the rest of the day and never threw them in the hamper. FYI, this is not some stupid irrelevant fact I'm including to make this story longer. It's relevant, I swear.

So the next morning I woke up the kids by screaming, "Yayyyyyyy, you're going back to school today!!!!!!!!!" And Zoey came out of her room wearing a giant frown AND her thermals from the day before with the big brown stain of hot cocoa down the front of them. Side note: If I had noticed she was wearing them to bed, I probably would have told her to change. Second side note: I probably did but she probably ignored me and wore them anyway.

ME: Get dressed for school!!
ZOEY: I am dressed.
ME: Nope, you wore those yesterday.
ZOEY: But it's cold out.

And I won't go into it in great detail, but let's just say there was a lot of anger and stomping and slamming of doors, but in the end I won. BTW, I also won in the beginning and the middle because I'm the mom. I made her change and she went to school wearing something different, and I told her if she wanted to wear her thermals again the next day, we could wash them that night.

Cut to the following morning.

ZOEY: Mommmm, did you wash my thermal underwear?!
ME: Nope.

Cue the anger and stomping and door-slamming again.

ZOEY: You lied!! You said you would wash them!!!!

ME: Zoey, I did not lie. I said WE could wash them, and
YOU never reminded me.

ZOEY: I forgot.

ME: Well, I forgot too.

So I dropped her off at school wearing something different, and as soon as I got home from dropping her off, I went up to my bathroom for some much needed alone time — wait, what's that? Something was taped to the mirror in my bathroom.

This.

Just in case your eyes are as crappy as mine and you can't read it, that little note says "Wash my cloths." Yup, Zoey left me a little note on my mirror that said "Wash my cloths." Awww, she even drew a cute little picture of a full hamper. Wait, not awww. Not awww at all. Yo, kiddo, I've got two things to say to you. Learn how to spell, and nooooooooo you did not just TELL me in a note to wash your clothes.

But yup, she did. Hmmm, what should I do about this? I thought for about .2 seconds before I knew exactly how I was going to respond. I walked straight into my bedroom and got out a pen and paper. Then I went to *her* bathroom.

I wanted to write "Wash your own *damn* clothes," but I resisted the urge to include the word "damn." Of course, I did include an adorable little illustration of a washing machine!! And when she got home from school and went into her bathroom, I was all the way at the other end of the house when I heard her gasp. And I smiled to myself. No, wait, that's a lie. I let out a huge guffaw.

> ZOEY: But, Mom! I don't know HOW to do my laundry
> by myself!!
> ME: Then I'm happy to teach you. Bring your hamper
> down to the laundry room.
> ZOEY: Okay, but later 'cause I'm doing something
> right now.
> ME: Okay.

And now it's later, and she's upstairs sleeping and she never brought her hamper down to the laundry room. Hmmm, I wonder whether I should be Mrs. McNiceymom and sneak into her room and grab her thermals and wash them for her. She would be soooo happy to wake up and find them all clean and ready to wear tomorrow morning. Maybe later. I'm busy doing something else right now—watching TV, sipping on my wine, and mentally preparing myself for the shouting fest tomorrow morning when she realizes we never washed her thermals.

OTHER MOTHER: Gasp, do you know what could happen if I let my six-year-old do the laundry?!!

ME: He could grow up to be a productive and self-sufficient human being?

OTHER MOTHER: I was going to say he could accidentally leave a tissue in his pocket and make a mess.

ME: (blank stare) Oh, the humanity.

The problem with buying sneakers with Velcro for your kiddos is that they'll be a grown-ass adult one day and they still won't know how to tie their own shoes.

The problem with buying sneakers with shoelaces for your kiddos is that you will literally be late to every single place you go for the rest of your lives and eventually you'll go insane and they'll cart you off in a straitjacket.

Velcro it is!

PARENTS: Go pick out a stuffie to bring on vacation.
KIDS:

- - - - - - - - -

I CAN EITHER:
A. Cook the eggs for breakfast while my kid is having screen time and it'll be faster and easier and cleaner.
Or B. Teach my kid to cook the eggs, and it'll be slower and harder and the kitchen will look like a bomb exploded.

THE CORRECT ANSWER IS:
C. Depends on what mood I'm in.

ONE LAST THING:
HERE'S WHEN YOU FIND OUT
I DON'T KNOW WTF I'M
TALKING ABOUT

This is the HUGE grain of salt I should have put at the front of this section. NONE of this shit's going to work. At least not for a lonnnnnnng time. As in AFTER your douchenuggets have left your house and live somewhere else and you go visit their new place and it looks halfway decent and you're like, "Wait, what, who lives here?! You can't be the same person who lived under my roof for 18 years."

Like I distinctly remember the look of utter shock on my parents' faces when they visited my first apartment and were like holy crap, it's clean-ish. I'm not surprised they were surprised. I mean, I was the kid who accidentally left a brown bag lunch on my bedroom floor and then crap kept getting piled on top of it until one day my mom made me clean my room and I found a lump of moldy sandwich oozing into my carpet so I just stacked a pile of textbooks on top of it so my mom wouldn't notice until I eventually went to college. I shit you not, this is a true story. And I have no idea what ever happened to that sandwich.

Anyways, my point is this. Despite everything I'm trying to teach my kids, it's not working. They still do a million things that drive me crazy.

- They leave empty boxes and cartons in the pantry.
- They constantly ask me to untie the knots THEY put in their shoelaces.
- They scream WIIIIPE MEEEEEE even though they were potty-trained like 200 years ago.
- They decorate the bathroom sink with hardened toothpaste like it's a blank canvas and they're Jackson Pollock.
- They treat my car like it's a trashcan.
- They treat my hand like it's a trashcan.
- They throw their clothes in the hamper inside out with the underwear still attached.
- They leave their disgusting damp towels on the floor in their rooms.
- They push their dishes across the island instead of carrying them to the sink.
- They clean their dressers by sweeping all their crap into a drawer.
- They throw *clean* clothes in the hamper until I tell them I'm going to make them start doing their own laundry, but I never actually make them so they keep doing it.
- They wet their toothbrushes just to fool me into thinking they brushed their teeth.
- They forget to flush the toilet, turn out the lights, make their beds, bring their dishes to the sink, open their shades, feed their pets, carry their backpacks in, take out their lunchboxes, take a bath, wash every crevice, brush their hair, brush their teeth, etc. etc. etc. etc. etc. etc. Seriously, there really aren't enough et ceteras in the world.

I mean, sure, occasionally I come into the kitchen and there's a dish by the sink and I think holy crap, someone call 1-800-VATICAN because a miracle just happened in my house. But 99.9999999 percent of the things I'm trying to teach my kids are not working. Yet. At least I hope *yet*. But here's the way I see it. One day it's gonna sink in, right? Like a moldy sandwich in a brown paper bag sinking into the carpet. It takes years, but eventually it's going to happen. Hopefully.

When my kids were little, I used to sing the cute clean-up song to get them to clean up a room. Now that they're older, I *still* sing the cute clean-up song. Only now it annoys the crap out of them so I purposely sing it super loud and they clean as fast as humanly possible just to get me to shut up. Success!!

—◦—

CHAPTER 2

Do Unto Others,
Even the Jerkwads

AHHH, REMEMBER THE GOOD OL' DAYS when you got to pick your kid's friends? You were like yeahhhh, I don't think we're gonna do a playdate with the kid who brought nunchucks to Gymboree class. But then kindergarten starts, and guess who your rugrat's hanging out with? Yup, little nunchuckerino. And he's teaching your kid all sorts of awesome things. Like how to throw spitballs and rocks and F-bombs. And you're sitting at home going aggghhhh, please don't destroy my sweet little innocent child.

But it's not up to you anymore. Because your sweet little innocent child is on his own now. And all you can do is hope that A) your kid is choosing to hang out with the nice people, B) your kid is *one* of those nice people, and C) your kid knows how to deal with the jerkwads. Because he will meet *plenty* of jerkwads. And he'll get to decide whether he turns the other cheek, kills them with kindness, or kills them with a sharp lethal weapon.

The good news is, if you teach him to be nice to everyone, everyone will be nice back. Oh shit, never mind, this isn't a *Brady Bunch* episode. But at least you'll know you probably won't get a phone call because he stole everyone's milk money, or called someone the "B" word, or shared a topless picture of his girlfriend on social media and ruined her life forever. And his. Because now he's on the national sex offenders list and can't live within 200 miles of a school, which really sucks because there are basically schools everywhere. Holy crap, this really isn't the *Brady Bunch* anymore, is it?

- - - - - - - - -

WTF YOU SHOULDN'T F'ING SAY IN FRONT OF YOUR F'ING KIDS

Shit, damn, fuck, crap, twatwaffle. These are words I've said in front of my kids. I mean, don't get me wrong, it's not like I *mean* to curse in front of them, but when you're walking down the stairs and you impale your foot on a LEGO that's basically a Ginsu knife in disguise, I dare you to remember to say Fudgsicle instead of the real F word. So yes, it's happened. Plenty. And there are people who will bitch and moan and say that it's never okay to curse like that in front of your douchenuggets. But here's the thing: Does the word *shit* really hurt anyone? I mean,

I know it's not super classy or anything, but neither is squirting the whipped cream canister straight into my mouth and I do that all the time. And honestly, I think there are wayyy worse things to say than an occasional F-bomb or sh-bomb. So without further ado, I present to you ten things I try not to say in front of my kids because I think they're wayyy worse than cursing:

1. I don't say the other F word.

I don't say I'm fat. I don't say my belly is fat. I don't say my thighs are fat. And I DEFINITELY don't say anyone else is fat. Someone else's body is none of my F'ing business. And I want my kids to look in the mirror and see a person with a big heart, not a big butt.

2. I don't say, "Boys don't cry."

Boys cry. All the time. They cry when they get hurt, they cry when someone dies, and they cry during sad movies and happy movies and Hallmark commercials. Don't get me wrong, if my boy falls down and isn't seriously hurt, I tell him to brush himself off and stop crying. Exactly the same thing I tell my daughter.

3. I never use any of the following words:

Cunt, bitch, slut, loser, idiot, retarded, that's so gay, freak, and pretty much any other word that exists purely to demean people.

4. I do not call colors boy colors or girl colors.

Colors do not have penises or vaginas. And neither do sports, clothes, or toys. Boys can take ballet, girls can love the color blue, and anyone can have a doll. As far as I'm concerned, if you call a truck a boy toy, that truck better have a big old wiener sticking out of it. In which case it's probably not appropriate for a girl OR a boy to play with.

5. I don't whisper quietly when I'm talking about race.

Whether someone is Black or white or Asian or Latinx or Green with Pink and Purple Dots isn't some deep, dark secret. If I act like it is, my kids are going to think it is. If I talk about race like it's all fine and dandy, guess what my kids are gonna take away from that? That it's all fine and dandy.

6. I don't say, "Awww, just let him give you a hug."

Because when my daughter is standing in the middle of a party her freshman year of college and the whole football team is yelling, "Suck it, suck it, suck it!!" I want her to hear another voice too. My voice in the back of her mind saying, "You don't have to."

7. I don't ask other moms if they work.

We all work. Like before I had kids I'd complain that I worked like 80- or 90-hour weeks. Now that I have kids I can tell you exactly how much I work every single week. One hundred and sixty-eight hours. And if you're wondering how I came up with that number, I just multiplied 24 by 7. The question isn't "Do you work?" The question is "Do you get paid in more than kisses and macaroni necklaces?"

8. I don't call people rich or poor in front of my kids.

Sometimes the richest people are the saddest people. And sometimes the people who live in a shack are the richest with happiness. And I'm trying to teach my kids that you can't judge people by how much money they have. There are rich people and there are poor people; for everyone else there's Mastercard. Wait, that doesn't make sense. But it sounds good!

9. I tryyyyy (and I stress the word try because old habits are hard to break) not to specify which gender they're gonna marry.

Instead of saying to my son, "One day you're gonna make some girl very happy," I say, "One day you're gonna make some*ONE* very happy." Because whether he's straight or gay or somewhere in between, it doesn't matter. The only thing that matters is that I like his spouse, that I like his spouse's parents, and that my son makes me lots of cute little grandbabies, either with his own equipment or someone else's.

10. I don't say, "You _____ like a girl."

Fill in that blank with pretty much any word (throw, run, bat, kick, think, dance, cry). As far as I'm concerned, there are only a few things in the world that people can do like a girl. So I guess I take it back. I might say, "You give birth like a girl" or "You menstruate like a girl," but I can't really imagine a scenario when I'd say that.

- - - - - - - - -

HOLDEN: Mom, the boys at school keep doing the "L" thing with their hand on their forehead.
ME: Whatta you mean? Like to say "loser"?
HOLDEN: Yes.
ME: Just tell them only losers say "loser." No, wait, that's not nice either. Why don't you make a different symbol back?

And we came up with a new response.

- - - - - - - - -

STICKS AND STONES MAY BREAK MY BONES BUT WORDS WILL COST THOUSANDS IN THERAPY

When Zoey was little and someone said something mean to her, you know what we taught her to say? "Sticks and stones may break my bones but words will never hurt me." Well, now that she's older I'm calling bullshit on our stupid naïve advice. You get poked in the eye with a stick, you go to the eye doctor and get that boo-boo fixed. But words? Mean words hurt like a mofo. And cause deep mental scars that are way more painful than any boo-boo.

So the other day when Zoey came home from school and she was treating me like dirt for no good reason, the first thing I said was, "Knock it off," and the second thing I said was, "What's the matter?" I was pretty sure something was wrong. And sure enough, her eyes started welling up. And that's when she told me about the girl at school who had suddenly joined her group of friends and was being super mean to her — telling Zoey she acts like a baby, telling her she can't play with them, telling her her clothing is weird, etc. etc. etc. Urrggh, I wanted to go to school and tell this girl to quit being a jackass, but that's not my job. *My* job is to focus on *my* kid, not someone else's.

> ME: So what'd you do when she said that?
> ZOEY: I just went and watched the boys play basketball instead.
> ME: Zoey, that is NOT what you need to do. You need to stand up for yourself.

But I could see it in her eyes. She was beaten down already. You know when you find a Cheerio on the ground that's been sucked on and discarded and now it's all dried out and shriveled up?

That's what her self-confidence looked like. This was too much for her to handle on her own. And that's when an idea popped into my head and I jumped on my computer and typed something into the Google search bar.

Comebacks for elementary school students

I kind of wondered whether anything would even come up, but stupid me. Of course stuff came up. Google knows everything (muahahahaha, this is total foreshadowing). So I started to put together a short list of the comebacks, and then I printed it out and knocked on her door.

ME: Hey, Zoey? I have something for you.

And I handed her the list of comebacks. Want to know how she reacted?

FYI, it's not blurry because I was drunk. It's blurry because the comebacks were so hilarious she was rolling around laughing. Anyways, she read them and I said a few mean things to her so she could try them out just for fun.

ME: Ewww, Zoey, your outfit is soooo gross.
ZOEY: If you're waiting for me to care, I hope you packed a lunch because it's gonna be a while.
Bwahahaha.
ME: Did you know that Melissa is inviting everyone to her birthday party except you?
ZOEY: Is your drama ever going to have an intermission?
Bwahahahahahahahaha.

And then the best part of all happened.

She came home from school a few days later and she was saying things like, "Oh, Mom, can I help you with that?" and "Mom, that color looks really good on you." She was being wayyyy too nice. I knew it had to be one of three things:

A. She murdered someone and was buttering me up so I wouldn't get too mad.
B. She was about to ask me to buy her something super expensive.
C. She had an exceptionally awesome day at school.

ME: Why are you so chipper?

And that's when she told me about her day. Apparently they were all sitting at the lunch table and this mean girl Ursula was going on and on about this other girl Lindsey.

> URSULA: . . . and did you know Lindsey's parents are getting divorced and they're going to have to move to a smaller house and blah bah blah more mean shit . . .

And the whole time Ursula was yapping away, this little girl Lindsey was sitting right there at the next table listening while Ursula just kept talking shit about her. Well, Zoey was sitting there the whole time getting madder and madder and madder until she finally couldn't help herself. She looked at Ursula and the words just poured out of her mouth.

> ZOEY: Unless your name is Google, stop acting like you know everything.

You know that sound when the record scratches and everything comes to a halt? THAT.

Zoey who's been sitting in the corner at the lunch table all year, Zoey who was in tears last week because someone called her clothing weird, Zoey who has amazing thoughts but who rarely raises her hand in class, MY Zoey said that.

Apparently Ursula's face looked like it turned into a tomato it was so red, and Lindsey looked at Zoey and gave her a huge smile, and Zoey winked at her. I had given Zoey that sheet of comeback lines to defend herself, but Zoey used it for something else. For someONE else. And she felt damn good about it. Her confidence was higher than I'd ever seen it.

A few days later I asked Zoey how things were going at school. I mean, I kinda suspected they were back to normal because she was consistently treating me at a level between dirt and gold, but I wanted to check in and be sure.

> ME: Has anyone been saying mean things to you again?
> ZOEY: Oh, no way, Mom. They know not to mess with *ME* now.

OMGeeeee, I think my heart almost burst with excitement. It worked! It worked!! Better than I could have ever imagined. No one is ever going to pick on Zoey again. Well, at least for a week or two. But the next time they try, she's gonna have something to say about it. Because of me. I mean, yeah, technically Google gave her the answer, but I'm feeling pretty damn good because I'm the one that thought to ask Google in the first place. Mic drop.

- - - - - - - - - -

TIP: Always carry a little change with you when you're going out with your kids. You never know when you're going to discover a fountain, or a gumball machine, or someone else who really needs it.

- - - - - - - - - -

PLAYDATES ARE AWESOME...
UNLESS THEY SUCK

You know what I love? When one of my douchenuggets invites a friend over to play and they play for three hours straight and I practically forget about them. It's total bliss, until I get a text from the mom and she's like, "I hope they're having fun!" and suddenly I realize ruh-rohhh, why is it so quiet upstairs? For all I know they jumped out the window and hitchhiked to Mexico or both of them fell out of the bunk bed and cracked their heads open at the same time. So I quickly bolt upstairs to make sure they're not lying in a pool of blood (uhhhh, just kidding if your kid has ever played at our house). But anyways, yes, those are the kids I invite over again. The ones who play so nice and quietly, they might be lying in a pool of blood.

But then there are the *other* playdates. The ones who require a little more attention. And I know I should just be grateful my kid's having fun, but ennnnhhhh, screw that. Because here's the thing. There are TWO reasons I invite kids over to play at our house. So my kid can have fun. And so I'm not their only source of entertainment from the time they get home from school until bedtime. Without further ado, drumroll please, badadadadadada, here are ten playdates who suck, some a little and some a lot:

1. Sir Snacks-a-lot
PLAYDATE: Holden's Mom, can I have some cookies?
ME: Of course!
PLAYDATE: Can I have something else now?

ME: Sure! Pretzels?

PLAYDATE: Mmmm. Now do you have any bacon?

ME: Ummmm.

PLAYDATE: Ham?

ME: (in my fake sweet voice) If you don't go play, you guys are going to run out of time.

PLAYDATE: Chips? Strawberries? Oooh, how about eggs?

ME: Doesn't your mom ever feed you?

PLAYDATE: Granola bars? Fruit Roll-Ups? Pudding? Chicken nuggets?

And so on and so on, until it's two hours later and he's literally licking the pantry shelves for residual crumbs.

Ding-dong! Oh, thank God.

ME: Here's your kid . . . and the grocery bill.

2. The kid whose house has no rules

ME: No snacks in the bedroom, girls.

PLAYDATE: At my house we can.

ME: Hey, girls, let's not draw on our skin.

PLAYDATE: At my house we can.

ME: Nope, we are not making purple slime on the white sofa, okay?

PLAYDATE: At my house we can.

ME: Next time you have a playdate, guess where you can have it?

PLAYDATE: Where?

ME: At your house we can!

3. The kid who doesn't want to do anything

PLAYDATE: I'm bored. What can we do?

ME: Why don't you play a board game? Or build a tent?
Or draw some pictures? Or play superheroes? Or go
play on the swing set? Or hang out with the gecko? Or
build with LEGOs? Or make up a play? Or put on some
costumes? Or make a car parade? Or have a lemonade
stand? Or build with Magna-Tiles? Or play basketball?
Or soccer? Or baseball?

PLAYDATE: What else?

4. The screen time addict

PLAYDATE: Can we watch TV?

ME: No TV.

PLAYDATE: Then where's your iPad?

ME: No iPad either.

PLAYDATE: Like you don't have one?

ME: We have one, we're just not playing with it now.

PLAYDATE: Is it out of juice?

ME: Nope, it has juice.

PLAYDATE: 'Cause if it's out of juice, we can play it while
it's plugged in.

ME: No iPad. Go play!!

PLAYDATE: Fine. Where's your Nintendo Switch?

5. The kid who convinces your angel to do bad shit. Literally.

PLAYDATE: Thanks for having me over!

ME: Thanks for teaching my kid the middle finger, the F word, how to pick bathroom locks, how to hock a loogie over the balcony, and how to poop in the houseplant.

6. Speaking of poopers

PLAYDATE: Wiiiiipe meeeeeeee!!!!

Oh, I'll wipe you all right. Right off our list of kids we have over for playdates. On second thought, you can come over again on one condition. Your mom gives you a colonoscopy prep kit the night before.

7. *The kid who wants to hang out with ME the whole time*

PLAYDATE: Will you play a game with us, Holden's Mom? Can we bake something, Holden's Mom? Will you color with us, Holden's Mom?

ME: Look, kid, this is *your* playdate, not mine. If it were *my* playdate, you would see two things. People my age, and wine.

8. *The friend who's not really a friend*

ME: Guess who's coming over today?

HOLDEN: Who?

ME: Cyrus!!

HOLDEN: Who's Cyrus?

ME: You knowww, Cyrus. From your class.

HOLDEN: I don't know him.

ME: You *literally* asked me to invite him over for a playdate last week.

HOLDEN: That was last week.

ME: So?

HOLDEN: We're not friends anymore.

Awesome.

9. *The hider*

ME: Jacob, your mom's here to pick you up!!!!

(nothing)

ME: Jacobbbbb!!!!!

(nothing)

ME: JACOB, COME GET YOUR SHOES ON!!!!!!
(nothing)

A small part of me is like, hells yeah, playdates at my house are so fun, kids don't want to leave. But most of me is like a bouncer at closing time: "You don't have to go home, but you can't stay here."

10. The liability
PLAYDATE: Let's take all the cushions off your couch, put them in a pile, and do flips off the balcony. Cannonball!!!!!

This ends in one of two ways. You hear what's going on and stop it before it happens. Or you call the mom to come meet you at the ER and *you* end up apologizing profusely to *her* for the rest of your life because *her* kid was the a-hole who wanted to be Evel Knievel. Yeahhh, that makes sense.

So there you go. You've also got the nose-picker, the kid who begs to stay for dinner every time, the mom who always shows up late, the tornado child who destroys your house, the dog-torturer, the kid who'd rather play with the sibling, etc. etc. etc. And hey, if your kid ever played at our house and I never invited them over again, it could be because they fit into one of these molds. Then again, it could also just be that I'm lazy and hardly ever remember to schedule playdates, so don't feel bad.

WHAT THE HECK DO
IKEA CUPS HAVE TO DO
WITH RACE RELATIONS?

About three years ago we bought some colorful plastic cups that we use all the time. They're from IKEA, which means they're super cheap and awesome, except for one thing. I can't help but pay attention to which color I'm giving to my kids. I know, I know, I'm not supposed to be all stereotypical about color, and I'm just supposed to grab the two cups from the top of the pile and put them on the table without thinking about it. But I don't. Because do you know what happens when I put the pink cup down in front of my son? A shitstorm of monumental proportions. And honestly I'm just too lazy to deal with that, so for the past year or so, if there's a pink cup or a purple one on top of the pile, I intentionally pull a different one from the middle. But I've decided to stop doing that. And here's why.

The other day we were in the car and Holden said something.

HOLDEN: I know someone who's Black.

Just to clarify, I don't remember what exactly we were talking about, but this wasn't totally random and it was in the context of our conversation.

ME: Oh yeah, who?
HOLDEN: Benji.
ME: Hmmm, well, buddy, he's actually not Black.
 He's Asian.

But it was interesting because clearly Holden noticed that there was something different about Benji's skin color. Some people say kids don't notice skin color and that it's taught, but I'm calling bullshit on that. Kids notice skin color. Like once when Zoey was a toddler she asked the man behind the deli counter if he was made of chocolate. Needless to say, I was mortified. I don't think kids look at someone of a different color and think the person is bad or anything, but I do think they notice sometimes, and we can keep our mouths shut and not talk about it because it's kind of an uncomfortable subject and we don't want to say the wrong thing and we're not supposed to notice color anyway, or we can be open about it and help our kids understand why diversity is a beautiful thing we should cherish. Not ignore.

So I've started to talk to my kids about it. And I'm trying to teach them that it's okay to notice someone's race, but that it's *not* okay to judge them for it. Because no matter what's on the outside, it's what's on the inside that counts. Thoughts, dreams, love, hate, beliefs, personality, kindness, humor, and an endless number of other things that make us who we are. You can notice someone's outside, but you can't really know them until you get to know their inside.

I know what you might be thinking right now. WTF? What does this have to do with the stupid IKEA cups? I'll tell you.

So the other day after Holden and I talked about race and trying not to judge people by their outside, I decided to reinforce our talk with a little demonstration. We were hanging out in the kitchen and he said he was thirsty, so I poured him a drink. Actually, I poured him *two* drinks. One in a pink cup and one in a green cup.

ME: Here you go, buddy. Which one do you want?
HOLDEN: Green!

Duhhh. He took a sip and I watched his eyes grow wide and his mouth pucker up and he looked like he was about to vomit and he spat the drink back out into the green cup.

HOLDEN: Blaggghhhh, what is that?!
ME: Tomato juice.
HOLDEN: Ewwwww. Why did you *make me* drink that?!
ME: I didn't. You picked the green cup. Want this one instead?

And I handed him the pink cup that was filled with yummy, sweet, delicious lemonade. He inspected it thoroughly before taking a hesitant sip and then smiling.

ME: Remember, buddy, it's what's on the inside that counts.

And I could see his little mind working hard, thinking about what had just happened.

HOLDEN: Like what we talked about earlier!
ME: Exactly.

Don't get me wrong. Do I think the IKEA cup challenge is going to solve all the world's racial injustices? Nope. But it's a start. And if I talk to my kids about race, and you talk to your kids about race, and other parents start talking to their own kids about race, then maybe things can change. Baby steps aren't gonna happen unless we take them.

Dear kid who punched Holden,

When Holden gets off the bus from camp every day, he's practically skipping. Even though he's sweaty and tired and completely worn out from playing, he bounces off the bus excited to eat a Popsicle with me on the porch and tell me how awesome his day was.

But not today.

Today his shoulders were slumping and his bottom lip jutted out and there were tears in his eyes. Why? Because you punched him. It hurt his stomach and his happiness.

I hope you're prepared to deal with me because I'm a fierce mama bear who will do everything in my power to protect my kiddos against anyone who hurts them. And you know what I'm thinking about doing right now? I'm thinking about marching straight over to your house to ring your doorbell and shake you by the shoulders and say, "How would you like it if someone punched you?" I'm thinking about having a very serious conversation with your mom and dad and letting them know that they're raising a bully. I'm thinking about calling up the camp and telling them to kick your butt to the curb and not give your money back because why should they since some other nice kid could have gone to camp instead of you.

But you're lucky. I'm thinking about doing them, but I'm not actually going to do them. Because I feel sorry for you. And even though Holden hates you and is scared of you, I'm trying to teach him to feel sorry for you too. You must be filled with a ton of sadness or anger or some other bad feelings and for some reason you think hurting other people around you will help you feel better. It won't. I mean, sure, misery loves company so you might appreciate the company, but it's not going to help you feel better. In fact, it will actually make you feel worse.

So I'll tell you what I am gonna do. I'm going to teach my son how to deal with you, and he might act a little differently than you're used to tomorrow. Like don't be surprised if he looks you straight in the eye when you get on the bus and says, "Hi," or asks you to sit in the seat next to him, or hands you a lanyard he made in arts and crafts, or smiles at you when you're both eating lunch, or waves to you across the soccer field. I'm guessing you'll be surprised because I'm assuming Holden's not the first kid you've punched, and I'm guessing most of the kids you've punched have either hated your guts or just avoided you altogether. Not my kid. My kid is under strict orders to kill you with kindness. So prepare to be killed. In a good way.

Last but not least, I'm leaving you with a warning. Do NOT take advantage of his kindness. Do NOT do it again. Because if you do, this mama bear will not be so nice the next time and she will attack. BIG TIME. I don't know how and I'll cross that bridge IF I get to it, but I'm hoping I won't get to it. I'm hoping, once someone in the world shows you a little kindness, that you'll realize how good it feels and that you'll want to feel that way more often. Fingers crossed.

This is your first warning and this is your last warning. Be glad you didn't mess with the wrong family. You messed with the right one. Ours.

Sincerely,
A mama bear who's *trying* very hard to
be more of a teddy than a grizzly

- - - - - - - - -

TIP: When someone is bullying my kiddo, I usually don't deal directly with their parents. For one, their parents are raising a bully so they might not have the best parenting skills, and two, I probably need my problem fixed sooner than they can fix theirs.

- - - - - - - - -

MY KIDS GET ALONG
EVERY SINGLE DAY...
FOR .3 SECONDS

I recently posted a picture of my sweet little kiddos cuddling on the couch together and I want to confess something. Here's how I got that picture. I set up the camera to record the living room the ENTIRE day. Then I sifted through 24 hours of footage and found the one 20-second period that they weren't tearing each other's limbs off and I posted it to every social media account I have. Seriously, if moms posted on the Internet what really happens at home, all our kids would go to jail.

You know how you had a second child so they could have a best friend for life? The key words in that sentence are "for life." As in "until one of them dies." Because let me ask you this. Does your best friend hum as loudly as possible just to drive you insane? Does your best friend purposely put their hand as close to you as possible just to piss you off? When you ask your best friend to stop doing something, do they purposely keep doing it louder and louder and LOUDER until you reach for the nearest weapon and murder them to death? I mean, occasionally when I hear about siblings who become best friends later in life, my reaction isn't relief. It's how the F did both of them survive to become adults?

So if you're wondering whether your children are normal for constantly fighting, the answer is yes. Siblings fight. *Constantly.* You didn't do anything to make them like that, and you can't do anything to make them not like that. All you can do is take solace in the fact that right this very second while you're sitting there thinking you might lose your F'ing mind because your kids won't knock it off, there are millions of other moms out there doing EXACTLY the same thing.

But if you're still worried about the ways your douchenuggets constantly battle it out, here are some NORMAL ways siblings fight:

When they get different presents

You know what's awesome? When Aunt Mildred comes to town and brings your kids toys. Two *different* toys. She gives little Sally a sloth stuffie and little Jack a narwhal stuffie and Jack starts crying his eyes out because he wanted a sloth, and that's when Aunt Mildred says, "Ohh, nooo, I knew I should have just gotten the unicorn stuffies because there were two of them," so now little Sally is bawling her eyes out because "Wahhhh, I want a unicorn stuffie!!!!" So then Jack says, "I'll take your sloth stuffie if you don't want it," and that convinces Sally that her sloth stuffie must be amazing since her brother wants it so then she says, "No way, I LOVVVVE my sloth stuffie," and then Jack starts crying because "She's rubbing it in!!" And you're speaking through gritted teeth the whole time telling your douchenuggets to knock it off and just be grateful for what they got. Even though you're not grateful for what you got either — two greedy kids who can't just be thankful for getting presents in the first place.

Family movie night

Ahhhh yes, let's all sit and watch a lovely holiday movie together as a harmonious peaceful family. This will be so nice. Ennnnh, bullshit. Because as soon as everyone has a seat on their own couch cushion, Sally tells Jack to stop crossing over the crack onto her couch cushion, which is basically the worst thing she can do because all Jack hears is, "If you want to annoy the crap out of Sally, just cross this line." And since Jack's main purpose in life is to torture his sister as much as humanly possible, this is like the best intel he can get and he's gonna slowly slide his foot across the divider line as often as possible throughout the entire movie and they're gonna fight like cats and dogs the whole time, and *It's a Wonderful Life* has just turned into *It's a Shitty Crappy Horrible Life*.

Killing each other in the car

WHAT YOU SAY: Come on, kids, put on your shoes and get in the car!!

WHAT THEY HEAR: Come on, kids, time to go to the Ultimate Fighting Championship!!

Seriously, it doesn't matter whether you're going on a three-day road trip to Aunt Edna's or a sixty-second drive down the street because you live in the suburbs and no one walks anywhere. The back seat of the car is basically the center cage at the UFC and the second your kids sit down and buckle their seatbelts, it's like the starting bell rang and they're ready to fight fight fight.

SALLY: MOMMMM, Jack won't stop leaning on me!!!
JACK: MOMMMMM, Sally keeps putting her finger near my face!!!!!
SALLY: MOMMM, Jack won't stop hitting me on purpose with his elbows!!!

If I could design a car, it would have one of those limousine dividers between the back seats — not between the front and back seats — between the BACK seats. Actually F that. Between the front and the back too. Basically I want to drive in an egg carton so we're each in our little cozy container and I will pay a crapload of money to the first car company that comes out with this.

Purposely annoying the other one

SALLY: (singing) A unicorn is beautiful and flying through the sky . . .
JACK: Can you stop singing, Sally?
SALLY: (singing every other word quietly) Unicorn hum hum hummm pretty . . .
JACK: Sally, stop!!!
SALLY: Humm humm hummmm hummm hummmmm . . .
JACK: SALLY!!
SALLY: Unicorn.
JACK: ARGGGHHHHHHHHHHH!!!!!!

And that's when Jack rips Sally a new one. Which is kinda hilarious since the last thing he needs is for Sally to have *another* orifice she can make more sounds out of.

Anything that can be destroyed

MOM: Wow, Sally, did you seriously build that all by yourself?

JACK: Ready or not, here I commmmme!!!!!

Awwww shit, apparently the purpose of LEGOs and blocks and Lincoln Logs and Bristle Blocks isn't to stimulate your child's brain and help turn them into the next world-renowned architect or engineer. Nope. These toys have two purposes: to injure parents' feet and to make children hate their younger siblings.

When anything is cut in half

No fair, her brownie is bigger!! No, his is bigger!! No, HERS is! No, HIS!!!!!!! And this is the moment Mom quickly picks up both brownies and shoves them both into her mouth IF Mom is like a total superhero badass. Me? I usually just tell them to knock it off but they don't so I end up giving up and walking away . . . to the nearest closet where I inhale the entire pan of brownies to help myself feel better. Which just makes me feel worse.

Sharing a bathroom

MOM: Who wants to take a bath first?!

JACK: Not me.

SALLY: I did it first last time!!!!

JACK: No, I did!!!

SALLY: I have to use the toilet.
JACK: I called it first!
SALLY: No, I'm first!!
MOM: Go use a different toilet!!
SALLY: No, I want THIS one!

JACK: I have to brush my teeth and Sally's been in there
　　　for hours.
SALLY: I'm pooping!!
JACK: You're watching your iPad!!
SALLY: While I'm pooping!!

SALLY: Jack touched my makeup!!
JACK: Sally put water in my toothpaste!!
JACK: Jack put my toothbrush in the trash!!
SALLY: Sally left her dirty underwear in the bathroom!!

And like a million other ways.

What show they watch on the iPad, who gets to sit in the better booster seat, whose room they use for a sleepover, who gets to put the candles in the menorah, who gets to light the candles, who lit the candles last night, who gets to sit in the window seat, who gets to sit in the aisle, where you're going for dinner, which movie you go to, who the mosquitoes bit more, who put the empty cracker box back in the pantry, who used the last of the milk and didn't get another carton, etc. etc. etc. etc. etc. etc. etc. etc. etc. etc. etc. Seriously, every mom is a lawyer, a referee, and a mediator, but mostly every mom just prays for one thing. That they love each other when they get older. You know, IF they don't kill each other first.

ZOEY: Mom, everyone has to do a presentation for the class
around a letter.
ME: Huh? Whatta you mean?
ZOEY: Like if you have "B" you can talk about basketball or
brains. And "C" could talk about cats.
ME: Oh, that's cool. What'd you get?
ZOEY: I picked the letter "K."
ME: "K?" Oy vey. That's a hard one. Karate? Kangaroos?
ZOEY: I have to think about it. It's not for a couple
of weeks.
ME: Okay.

Then yesterday I pick her up from school and she comes running into the car.

ZOEY: Mom, it was my presentation today!
ME: Oh shit, I totally forgot. I'm so sorry, honey!! Can you
make it up tomorrow maybe?
ZOEY: I didn't forget.
ME: Really? You remembered?
ZOEY: Yes, I did it!
ME: On what?
ZOEY: On kindness for kids. Two K's!! I paired everyone
up with someone else in the class, and don't worry I kept
all the boys apart so they wouldn't be silly, and then they
had to say kind things to each other. And then I gave
people rewards for being kind.

ME: Seriously, Zoey? That's amazing.
ZOEY: Thanks!

Sometimes when I feel like everyone's fighting and the world is falling apart, I look at our children and I think everything's gonna be okay.

DON'T YOU JUST LOVE WHEN STRANGERS OFFER YOU UNSOLICITED ADVICE?

The other day I'm standing in the parking lot at Starbucks waiting for my kids to get out of the car. Side note: Why do I have to tell my kids to get out of the car anytime we get somewhere? Hellllooooo, the car is parked and turned off. Wouldn't you think that would automatically signal them to get out? But nope. So I'm standing there super annoyed and yelling at them to get out for the nine hundredth time when a woman gets out of the car next to me.

I barely even notice her out of the corner of my eye until I realize she's standing there just staring at us. I turn to look, thinking it must be either:

A. Someone who knows me

Or B. Someone who literally froze to death where she's standing because it's like negative ten degrees out

I'm wrong. Just by the look on her face, I can tell that she's C. One of those perfect mommies who wants to tell me I'm doing it wrong. And FYI, if you're wondering what "it" is, it's not one thing. I mean, yeah, technically she's only going to tell me one thing I'm doing wrong at that moment, but I guarantee you this is the kind of woman who goes around telling moms they're doing alllllll kinds of shit wrong. (Read the following in a British accent — nothing against British people, but your accent just sounds snootier than ours.) "You need to scold your children more, your car seat is too small, you're buckling them wrong, you really need to cover up when you breastfeed, you should give them baths every day, do you want your children to get cancer, etc. etc. etc."

Anyways, I'm standing there watching my douchenuggets move slower than molasses (they could race a glacier right now and the glacier would win) when the woman finally opens her pie hole.

RANDOM KNOW-IT-ALL: I just want to make sure you know that book could kill your child.

Huh? What book? I look in the car and see it on the floor.

ME: *Curious George and the Puppies*?

Seriously, is this book dangerous propaganda or something? I'm picturing a bunch of angry people with pitchforks throwing it into a giant bonfire.

RANDOM KNOW-IT-ALL: If you have an accident
that book could turn into a projectile and literally kill
a child. I'm just telling you because I care about your
children.

Ahhhhh, yes, for a minute there I was wondering what she
has against mischievous monkeys that cause problems and then
get rewarded when the problems are solved. But I just love the
way she says it, as if I must not care about *MY* children as much
as she does. As I'm standing there debating how to respond, she
opens her mouth again.

RANDOM KNOW-IT-ALL: It happened to a toddler in
my friend's town.

Yes, because it happened once to a child somewhere far away
we should all be very scared it's going to happen again. But seriously, lady, my kid was reading a book in her car seat and you're
going to tell me it's dangerous? People give their kids grapes in
the car. People give their kids iPads in the car. People who live in
rural towns let newborns drive heavy machinery on empty farm
roads. But MY kid chooses to read a piece of intellectual litera-
ture (this is called hyperbole) and you're going to tell me I'm doing it wrong? I mean, come on, I was just steering my steering
wheel with my knee so I could unwrap a cheese stick and blindly
pass it back to my son (a true skill), but you want to rip me a new
one because my daughter was reading a book in the car.

Anyways, do you know how I responded to her? I reached into my minivan, picked up the book, and told her to bend over so I could shove it where the sun don't shine. Nahhhhh, just kidding. That's what I wanted to do.

But nope. Here's what I did.

I strapped on the biggest shit-eating grin you can possibly imagine and I turned to that lady and said in the sappiest voice I could muster up, "Thank you sooooo much." The words were nice, my voice was nice, my kids totally thought I was being nice and saw me set a good example, but if you read between the lines you could see my middle finger sticking straight up in the middle of them. And then I headed into Starbucks with my kids. Did she know I was being sarcastic? No idea. Don't care. It's taken me years to learn this but I finally have. These people aren't worth my time. Whether they actually mean well or they just want to feel superior to me, who gives a shit? I can let their words eat me up inside and dream about all the clever comebacks I should have said, or I can just smile and telepathically tell them to F off and move on. I choose the latter.

I went inside, ordered a gigantic much-needed coffee, yelled at my kids for putting their grubby little fingers all over the food in the case, and I never thought about that woman again.

and the princesses lived happily ever after.

There's nothing wrong with a prince marrying a princess at the end. I just don't want it to be the ONLY story my kids see.

ZOEY: Mom, today I read a bad word in a book.
ME: Oh no. What word?
ZOEY: Shit.
ME: Yeah, that's not really a word you should use.
ZOEY: I know. I'll only say "shit" around you.
ME: Sounds good. And really there are words that are way worse. *Shit's* not all that bad.

ZOEY: Yeah, because we all do it.

ME: Do what?

ZOEY: You know, take a shit.

ME: True, but really I think mean words are way worse than words like "shit."

ZOEY: Like what?

ME: Like "loser" and "stupid." Or there are some *really* mean words people call Black people and Jewish people.

ZOEY: What are they?

ME: Hmmm, I'm not sure I want to even say them.

ZOEY: Okay, then can you teach me some words that are on the same level as "shit"?

ME: Hahahahaha.

ZOEY: No, seriously, teach me some.

ME: You won't say them?

ZOEY: Only with you.

ME: Okay. Asshole.

ZOEY: Assle? Am I saying it right?

ME: No, ass hole.

ZOEY: What's ass mean?

ME: Well, it's your butt.

ZOEY: Ewwww. So it's the hole in your butt?

ME: Exactly.

So yup, I taught my kid the word "asshole." And what it means. But hey, the way I see it, better me than some other assle.

- - - - - - - - -

YET ONE MORE REASON DISNEY IS THE BEST THING SINCE SLICED BREAD

Dear Disney,

Thank you. No seriously, THANK YOU. I mean, sure, there's the obvious shit I can thank you for, like the fact that I've been able to do laundry and make dinners and take showers and go poop for the past ten years while you've entertained my douchenuggets over and over again. But there's something a little less obvious I want to thank you for too. Thanks for helping me make my kids better people.

The way *Dumbo* taught my kids that being born a little different can actually be a good thing. And that even if people make fun of you for it, you can turn your differences into something special.

The way *Cinderella* taught my kids that if you keep working hard and you keep being nice, good things will eventually come your way. Karma.

The way *Peter Pan* taught them that thinking happy thoughts can lift you up, so you're better off seeing the glass half full because it'll take you farther in life.

The way *Snow White* taught them that whistling while you work makes doing annoying chores go a little faster.

The way *Beauty and the Beast* taught them you're better off falling in love with someone whose inside is more beautiful than their outside (although I'm still begging you, shorten the movie and eliminate the part where he turns into Fabio at the end).

The way *Finding Nemo* taught them to make new friends but keep the old, and always stay with your group on a field trip.

The way *Honey I Shrunk the Kids* taught them not to mess around with their parents' stuff unless they ask permission.

The way *Pinocchio* taught them people will know if you're lying.

The way *Coco* taught them that other cultures aren't weird. They're amazing.

The way *Star Wars* taught them princesses can be total badasses.

And like a million other awesome lessons.

Because here's the thing. Even though I could easily sit down and tell my kiddos all this stuff, they won't listen. Like if I said, "Don't elope with the first hot guy you meet," my kid who has *selective* listening would only hear a few of the words — "Elope with hot guy" — and I'd get a collect call from Vegas begging me to come pick up her just-married/just-divorced ass. But for some reason my kids listen when the message is delivered through super skinny animated sisters with disproportionately large eyes and a chipper snowman who loves summer.

So thank you. Thank you for helping me nourish my little beans and grow them into nice, kind, strong, open-minded, happy, loving, adventurous but not too adventurous, hard-working humans.

Love love LOVE,
A mom who has many
good reasons to love Disney

- - - - - - - - -

HOLDEN: Mom, do you want this Jelly Belly?
ME: Sure!
HOLDEN: Wait, what flavor is it?
ME: Toasted marshmallow.
HOLDEN: I want it back.
ME: Then why'd you give it to me?
HOLDEN: Because it has brown spots on it.
(I pop it in my mouth)
HOLDEN: Mommmm, I said I wanted it back.
ME: You shouldn't judge something by the way it looks.

Mmmmmmmm, deeeelicious.

- - - - - - - - -

ONE LAST THING:
THE FINE PRINT AT THE
BOTTOM OF THIS SECTION

Remember how I ended the story about the bully who was picking on Zoey with a mic drop? Picture me tiptoeing back onto the stage right now to sheepishly pick up that microphone. Because even though the comeback line totally worked, apparently it expired after about two weeks when that persistent bully came back like a chronic hemorrhoid.

> ME: Anything happen at school today?
> ZOEY: (frowning) Ursula.

It took years and years of bad shit to turn Ursula into the little crabapple that she is, and one comeback line ain't gonna change her into a sweetie pie. And I keep telling Zoey that she needs to let Ursula's assholiness roll off her back because it has nothing to do with her but she's not buying it. Because even if you feel bad for Ursula, it still hurts when she calls you a crybaby, or purposely leaves you out at recess, or makes fun of your outfit in front of your friends. And Zoey's self-esteem can only take so much. So Zoey goes back and forth between bombarding Ursula with comeback lines and kindness, but Ursula is Ursula and there's only so much Zoey can do.

And then there's Holden. My sweet little innocent, cuddly boy. Guess what he did this year? Punched someone in the bathroom. Yup, the principal called and told me what happened, and I could have been one of those moms who was like no way, not my kid, he's not the kind of kid who'd punch someone. But I wasn't. I was the kind of mom who begged the school to come down hard on him, and then I made Holden write a lonnnnggg apology note, and then I took away screen time for a month (NOT a typo). He's been a model student ever since. So far.

But I'm not stupid. He'll F up again. And so will Zoey.

Not because they're bad kids, but because sometimes *good* kids do *bad* things. And sad kids do bad things. And angry kids do bad things. And frustrated kids. And bored kids. And peer-pressured kids. *ALL* kids do bad things sometimes. They're not bad kids. Even the ones who do bad things over and over and over again, like Ursula or the camp bully. They're just upset or hurting or abused or lonely or wired differently or undisciplined or something else. And if they're doing something wrong, there's a good chance it's because some grownup isn't teaching them what's right. So we shouldn't hate them or be mean to them or think we can change them. All we can do is teach our kids how to deal with them. And cross our fingers that it's gonna work. And PRAY they don't get too hurt in the meantime.

- - - - - - - - -

I hear people say it all the time. When you have children, you can't have nice things anymore. But I totally disagree. You can have nice things. The nice things *ARE* your children.

———○———

CHAPTER 3

Picasso's Mom Didn't Tell Him to Draw the Eyes in the Right Place

WHEN PICASSO WAS A RUGRAT, do you think his mom said, "Pablo, please go put on some matching socks?" and "Pablo, can't you color the sky blue like everyone else?" Probably not. Because seriously, if Picasso's mom tried to make him do things like everyone else, we probably wouldn't even know his name.

Amazing people don't blend in. They stand out because of the way they dress (Lady Gaga), design (Gianni Versace), break molds (Ruth Bader Ginsburg), think (Albert Einstein), paint (Pablo Picasso), or any number of ways they express themselves. Encouraging kids to be creative is crazy important. I mean, when my rugrat comes out of her room wearing her Greek goddess Halloween costume with a furry vest and a pink cowboy hat, I can tell her to go back in and change into something more normal, or I can say, "Wow, you look AMAZING!" And to be honest, who am I to tell her to go back inside and change anyway? I wear pajama pants, granny panties, and a fanny pack. I mean, not out in public . . . well, unless I'm feeling lazy. Which is pretty much every day.

HOLDEN: Mom, can I wear my new outfit to
    school today?
ME: It's a bathing suit.
HOLDEN: So can I?
ME: No, buddy, you can't wear a bathing suit to school.
HOLDEN: But Zoey's wearing pajamas.
ME: Because it's Pajama Day in her class.
HOLDEN: Mom, I forgot to tell you something.
ME: What?
HOLDEN: It's Bathing Suit Day in my class.
ME: (blank look)
HOLDEN: (bats eyelashes)
ME: Fine.

TWENTY THINGS TO DO
TO HELP MAKE
YOUR KIDS CREATIVE

I open up a Pottery Barn Kids catalog and I'm like, how the hell do these kids have such pristine bedrooms? Oh yeahhhhh, because there's nothing in them. No trophies, no guinea pigs, no science fair medals, no random jars of slime, no Happy Meal toys, no stuffies they won playing Whack-a-Mole, no LEGO sets they insist on displaying, no glow-in-the-dark stars on the ceiling, and definitely no tape on the walls. I mean, I get it, when I was preggers for the first time, I spent hours and hours figuring out how to decorate Zoey's bedroom perfectly. My hubby would move a throw pillow and I'd be like AGGGHHHH, NOOOOO, the pink pillow goes in front of the orange one and the cow stuffie goes in the middle and the toys on the shelf are just for decoration so do not touch them.

That lasted about .3 seconds before I realized something. It's a room, not a museum, and they're kids, not dolls. And they need to express themselves — whether your kid's a neat freak who matches her socks to her underwear, a crazy kindergartner who insists on wearing a Zorro mask wherever he goes, or the girl who wants black walls in her room because she's a Steelers fan.

So if you want your kid to be a perfect little doll who wears pinafore dresses and behaves like she's in a commercial and lives in a Pottery Barn catalog, please go buy one of those freaky dolls that looks like a real child. But if you want your kiddo to be an independent free thinker who doesn't always look like she has her shit together, here are a few pointers:

1. Let them put tape on their walls. Don't think of it as ruining the paint. Think of it as encouraging their creativity.
2. Throw them in the backyard without an activity so they learn that mud and leaves and sticks and hills are some of the best toys ever invented.
3. Let them wear whatever they want, as long as they're not gonna freeze to death, sweat to death, or make a private part not so private.
4. Look at the bright side when they want to wear their Halloween costume in February — you didn't pay for an outfit they'll only wear one day of the year.
5. Hang up their artwork when *they* think it's amazing. Even if you don't.
6. Let your boy wear nail polish if he wants to. Blue, black, silver, pink, purple. If people pick on him, he'll have two options — not wear it anymore, or not take their shit.
7. Let your girl cut her hair short if she wants. If people think she's a boy, so what. As long as she thinks she's a badass.
8. Have at least one place in your house where they can accidentally spill paint or make a mess and you won't freak out. This is good for them AND you.
9. Embrace magical shit like Elf on the Shelf and the Tooth Fairy and the Donut Fairy. And if you don't know what the Donut Fairy is, she's this magic fairy who hides donuts for EVERYONE in the house so duhhh, it's obviously a good thing to embrace.

10. Encourage them to build LEGOs WITHOUT a set sometimes. Great for their brains and your wallet.

11. Resist the urge to tell them to color inside the lines. Creative people don't just color what's in front of them.

12. Find blank canvases wherever you can — a napkin, a cardboard box, a cupcake, a foggy window. Just hopefully not your walls or furniture.

13. As much as it drives you crazy and makes your mornings harder, embrace Crazy Hair Day and Crazy Sock Day and Davy Crockett Day. (I shit you not, this was a real day I had to embrace. Luckily we owned a coonskin hat. NOT.)

14. When your kid asks you to rinse out a milk carton so they can do something with it, go ahead and roll your eyes. And then rinse it out for them.

15. After you tell your kid a story, ask him to tell YOU one.

16. When they build a fort in the living room, leave it there for a few days. It's not just about building the fort. It's about playing in it.

17. Instead of bringing the iPad with you, bring some markers and paper. When your kid says, "Nooo, I want the iPad!!" just say something annoying like, "Then why don't you draw a *picture* of an iPad?!"

18. If they make you a pipe cleaner crown or a macaroni necklace or a construction paper purse, wear it like it's the most beautiful thing on earth. At least until they go to school.

19. Teach them that making videos can be even more fun than watching them.

20. Schedule "nothing to do" time on your calendar. They'll always find something to do.

ZOEY: Thank the gods.
ME: I think you mean thank God.
ZOEY: No, I don't. Thank the gods. I believe in Greek
    mythology.

All righty then, I stand corrected.

WTF ARE YOU WEAR —
UHHHH, I MEAN, DON'T YOU
LOOK FANTABULOUS!!

So you're standing in the kitchen packing lunchboxes when your kid comes in wearing, wait, WTF is that? That's not the pretty pink dress you picked out for her to wear today. That's, ummmm, uhhhh, I don't know *what* that is. Plaid pants with a paisley shirt and a furry vest and gold cowboy boots. I mean, she looks like Raggedy Ann on acid went to a dude ranch. And you have two choices:

Say something like, "Hmmm, what happened to the pretty dress I put out for you?"

Or...

"Did we just land in New York City because I'm pretty sure I must be at Fashion Week?!"

And here's the thing. If you go with option 1, you're basically saying, "Are you sure you want to wear that? Because it looks like shit." But if you go with option 2, you're basically saying, "Look at you, you forward-thinking badass."

I mean, no, not in so many words, but kids pick up on what we're thinking. And soooo much of their self-confidence comes from that. Don't get me wrong, there have been plenty of times I've F'ed up in this department.

ME: I'm just a little worried that outfit is gonna give people seizures.

ME: Hmmm, do you think maybe the glasses are a little much?

ME: Hey, Zoey, Germany called. They want their beer garden outfit back.

ME: Ummmmm.

ME: What do you want me to pack in your lunchbox,
sweetie pie? Acid or shrooms?

And every time I question her, I feel like crap after I do it. I mean, I'm always saying I want a girl who can think for herself and doesn't have to follow what everyone else is doing. Which means I need to let her express herself without judging. But sometimes I forget and there's this little voice that creeps into my head. The one that whispers, "What if people make fun of her?" "What if she stands out so much that she can't find her niche?" "What if people think *I* picked out her outfit?" "What if she keeps dressing crazy for the rest of her life and she can't make friends or get a job or walk down the street without people staring at her?"

And then one day my bad thoughts came true. The little voice was right. Last week Zoey came home from school and said the words I've been dreading for a long time.

ZOEY: A girl at school asked me why I always dress weird.

I could see how much it hurt her. And I'll tell you what went through my head. WHO said that to you?!!! Was it Brunhilda?!! Urrrgghh, it's always Brunhilda. Tomorrow I'm going to hide behind a bush at recess and if she says anything again I'm going to jump out and eat her alive. Yup, my mama bear instincts kicked in big time. But then I remembered something. I'd be arrested.

So I told Zoey to ignore Brunhilda. That she's clearly hurting on the inside and taking it out on other kids and *trying* to make them feel bad like her. And Zoey nodded and agreed but I couldn't help but feel like the conversation wasn't enough. That there's always going to be some Brunhilda or Gertrude or Bartholomew who's going to purposely make her feel bad about her clothing choices. But what else could I have said? And 19 hours later it hit me.

The next day I was sitting at a traffic light when something popped into my head. The RIGHT answer. It had nothing to do with Brunhilda. It was all about Zoey. And when I went home that night, I said what I should have said in the first place.

ME: So Brunhilda called your clothing choices weird?
    Wanna know who's weird, Zoey?
ZOEY: Brunhilda?
ME: No, she's dull. I'll tell you who's weird. Alexander McQueen, Lady Gaga, Pink, Roberto Cavalli, Madonna, Albert Einstein, Katy Perry. The next time Brunhilda or any other little lemming calls you weird, you say, "Thank you." And you wear that weird badge with pride. Weird means you think for yourself. Weird means you don't just copy everyone else. Weird means you're a leader, not a follower. Weird means you are awesome. F'ing awesome. And don't you forget it.

I mean, Zoey probably stopped listening to me halfway through my speech because kids basically have the attention span of a gnat on Red Bull, but I think she got the gist of it. I hope.

The world is full of regular people. People who just want to wear what the mannequin is wearing. And there's nothing wrong with that. But if you've got a kid who thinks out of the box, who marches to the beat of their own drum, who wears a necktie as a headband or crazy mismatched socks every day or their hoodie backwards on purpose, then congratulations. You're raising someone who's interesting. And when they come into the kitchen wearing something that makes you think, "Oh shit," try to remember, that's a good thing.

- - - - - - - - -

When Zoey was little, maybe in kindergarten or first grade, so many of the girls in her class were getting their ears pierced and Zoey asked her dad whether he thought she should get hers pierced too.

HUBBY: I think you look beautiful.

From that moment on, whenever I asked her if she wanted her ears pierced, or if anyone else did, she'd say the same thing.

ZOEY: Nope. I look beautiful the way I am.

Until the day we were all at a carnival outside the mall and Zoey suddenly said, "Can we go in there and get my ears pierced?" I asked, "Are you sure?" And she said, "Definitely."
So our whole family went inside the mall. And once it was done she looked at her daddy and asked what he thought.

HUBBY: I think you look beautiful.

And that's when I realized something. The first time he said it, he wasn't saying "I think you look beautiful *without* your ears pierced." He was saying he thinks she looks beautiful no matter what. With or without earrings. With or without tattoos. With short hair or long hair or blue hair or no hair. And she will always feel beautiful because her daddy says she is.

- - - - - - - - -

ME: Hey, Zoey, do you want me to do your hair over so it's a little, uhhh, neater?

ZOEY: Nope, I like it like this. Can you take a picture so I can see the back?

Oh, thank God. That'll bring her to her senses.

ME: Sure! And then you can decide if you want me to redo it.

(I show her this picture)

ZOEY: Wow. I mean, wowww.

ME: You want me to redo it?

ZOEY: Are you crazy?! Nooo. I mean, it's a little formal, but I really like how the three ponytails all come into one. Right?!

ME: Oh yeah, definitely.

SCREEN TIME IS YOUR FRENEMY

So the other day, I was chitchatting with a friend about her vacation and I asked how her rugrats did on the flight.

> FRIEND: They had their iPads the whole time so of course they were fine. I don't know *what* parents did on flights before iPads.
> ME: Drank a lot.

That's what I said out loud. But in my head I was thinking, "You know what kids did on airplanes before iPads? Colored pictures, read books, played cards, looked at the clouds, played I Spy, chatted, fought over the window seat, and coughed if they were sitting near the smoking section." Not kidding. If you're as old as I am, you might remember that airplanes once had smoking sections, which is pretty hilarious since a plane is basically just one long oval room without any walls. But I digress.

Anyways, back in the day, kids had to entertain themselves and use their little brains to come up with creative stuff. Which might have been a little harder and the airlines might have sold more of those mini bottles of alcohol, but there's something to be said for boredom. Boredom makes you come up with some creative shit.

Do NOT get me wrong. I'm as guilty as the next parent when it comes to iPads on the airplane. If I'm gonna be stuck in a metal capsule with my douchenuggets and 150 complete strangers who hate my guts the second they see me board with kids, I'm all about the iPad, or pretty much any device that will get us from point A to B without losing our shit along the way. You wanna watch six straight hours of *Paw Patrol* until your brain morphs into oatmeal, kid? Go for it. I mean, pretty much the only rules I have for my kids on the airplane are: do not spit out your gum anywhere but a napkin or my hand, always wear your headphones so the rest of the plane doesn't have to listen to Caillou or Peppa Pig or Atari beeps, and don't kick the seat in front of you. And really the people sitting around us STILL have to wear earplugs so they don't have to listen to me screaming, "Stop kicking the seat in front of you!!" the whole flight.

But here's the thing. Once we're off the airplane, there is screen time and there is *non* screen time. You know, those times of the day when I flip the off switch and my kids get all pissed off and I'm like, deal with it. Because when I look around, kids these days are constantly entertained. OMG, did I just say *kids these days*? Holy crap, I've turned into an old fogy. OMG, did I just say *old fogy*? Excuse me while I go check myself into an assisted living facility. But seriously, kids these days are never bored.

DOUCHENUGGET: Mommmm, I'm borrrred, what can
   I do while we're waiting 60 seconds for my Happy Meal?
DOUCHENUGGET'S MOM: Here, play a game on
   my phone.

Just the other day I was in the grocery store and I noticed that the little cars that toddlers ride in now have a TV inside. As in a REAL television set. Wha-WHAT?!!! I know this sounds awesome if you have a toddler and you're trying to shop for a week's worth of food and how can I blame parents for taking the easy way out when it's sitting right there, but I genuinely worry that these kids will never be able to develop an original thought on their own if someone doesn't unplug them once in a while.

DOUCHENUGGET'S MOM: Sweetie pie, put your shoes on!! We have to go grocery shopping!!

DOUCHENUGGET: But I wanna watch TV!!!

DOUCHENUGGET'S MOM: You can, sweetums! Just pause the iPad and we can watch TV in the minivan on the way to the grocery store where you can watch TV in the cart and then TV on my iPhone in the checkout line and then in the minivan on the way home again.

Does this mean I'm against screen time? Hell no. I LOV-VVVVVVVVVVVVE (really there aren't enough V's in the world) screens. I love my TV. I love my iPad. I love my computer. I love my iPhone. I love movies, shows, videos, all of it. But wanna know what happens when you flip OFF the screen in the Piggly Wiggly? Your kid throws a major tantrum and everyone stares at you and you start speaking through gritted teeth. "Taylor Alison Swift, if you don't knock it off right now they're gonna kick us out of this store!"

But wanna know what happens after she knocks it off? You're walking through the aisles and grabbing food when suddenly little Taylor Swift starts making up a song and by the time you're checking out at the register, she's written the lyrics to "Shake It Off" (FYI, I have no F'ing idea if Taylor Swift wrote "Shake It Off" in the Piggly Wiggly or even if her mom shopped at the

Piggly Wiggly, but I do know her middle name is Alison because I just looked it up).

My point is this. If little Tay Tay's mom let her watch the iPad all the time, she probably wouldn't be a humongous success. So when you're on the airplane, by all means, let your kids watch as much screen time as humanly possible. But once you're on the ground, make sure they're unplugged once in a while so they have to be creative and come up with stuff to entertain themselves. Who knows, maybe your kid will become the next Taylor Swift, or Henri Matisse, or Frank Lloyd Wright, or Amy Schumer, and make a crapload of money and buy you lots of awesome shit. Not that that's the goal or anything (I'm lying, it totally is).

- - - - - - - - -

HOLDEN: I wish Dad were gone so I can marry Mom.
ZOEY: And I get Dad.
HOLDEN: Wait, no, I want to marry Dad. (pause) I'm gay.

My hubby and I just sat there and didn't bat an eye.

ME: Okay.
HUBBY: Sounds good.

It was such a HUGE moment. Not because Holden said he was gay. He's little and doesn't understand that yet. It was huge because of our reaction. Or lack thereof.

- - - - - - - - -

TEN COOL THINGS YOUR KIDS CAN DO WHEN THEY DON'T KNOW WHAT TO DO

"I'm borrrred. There's nothing to do. I already colored. I don't want to read. Why can't I watch TV? How about I just hang out in whatever room you're in and start whistling a super annoying song while stabbing you in the butt with a light saber?"

Seriously? Seriously?!! I swear we own 9,000 toys and games and books and all sorts of stuff, but my kid claims there's nothing to do.

So over the years, I've managed to come up with a decent list of creative shit your kids can do with just random stuff you have lying around the house. Easy peasy stuff to keep them occupied. So here goes.

1. *The drink challenge*

I'm sure you're like WTF is the drink challenge? It's super simple. Tell your kids to leave the room (my favorite part!). Then you get out ten cups and fill them with mystery liquids from the fridge. Regular stuff like OJ or milk, weird stuff like soda water or soup, deeeeelicious stuff like chocolate milk or Coffee-Mate, and one cup with something really gross in it. Maybe pickle juice, or soy sauce, or salad dressing. Blagggh. Then you blindfold your kids and they take a sip, and on the count of three they all yell out what they think it is. Or if it's pickle juice, they start gagging and freaking out and crying and you feel kinda bad, even though it's pretty hilarious.

2. A plain boring empty box

You know what I love? When I buy my kid a super expensive toy and they end up playing with the box. So these days I skip the middleman and I just hand them an empty box. At first they look inside and they're like, "WTF, Mom, it's empty." But an hour later, they've created a puppet show or a clubhouse or the Taj Mahal and I'm like awwww shit, now they're never gonna let me throw that box away.

3. A photography walk

ME: Wanna go on a walk?

KIDS: BO-ring.

ME: Wanna go on a photography walk?

KIDS: Yesssss!!! (pause) Mom, what's a photography walk?

I mean, it's just a walk, but you hand your kid a camera, and suddenly a boring walk is exciting — whether they're taking a super close picture of a pile of rocks or looking at a tree from a different perspective.

4. The blindfolded drawing challenge

Give each kid a piece of paper and a marker, and blindfold them. Then just shout out something for them to draw. A dog. Go. A superhero. Go. A house. GO! And they have to draw it without looking. When they're done they get to take their blindfold off and see what they drew.

> KID: Mom, look, the windows are on the chimney!!!
> ME: Bwahahahahaha. That's almost as hilarious as the fact that I ate an entire sleeve of Girl Scout cookies while you were blindfolded and you had no idea!

5. A ridiculously simple
scavenger hunt—inside or outside

I mean, RIDICULOUSLY simple. Like take 60 seconds to type 30 words of objects you know are in or around your house, and then hand it to your kids:

Black hat
Paper clips
A pink LEGO
Plaid underwear
Etc. etc. etc.

It'll take them at least 15 minutes to find it all. That's 15 blissful minutes of not hearing "I'm borrrredddddd."

6. Still life

Sure, you could take them to Michaels to pick out an expensive art project that will occupy like two seconds of their time and make you freak out because it's a huge mess, or you can do this. Pick up five inanimate objects from around your house. Flowers, a vase, a bowl, fruit, knickknacks, paddywhack, give a dog a bone, shit what was I saying? Oh yeah, get five objects, hand your kiddo a piece of paper and some markers, and let them draw a still life. That's how Picasso got started, ya know? He was hitting his sister so he lost screen time and didn't have anything to do.

7. Dinner

Nahhhh, I don't mean just feed them dinner. Unless it's 4:59, in which case go ahead. Nope, I mean THEY are in charge of dinner.

ME: Hey, Holden and Zoey, I want you to be in charge
of dinner tonight. You need to create a menu, be the
waiters, and do the whole thing without me.
HOLDEN AND ZOEY: How do I —
ME: Uh-uh-uhhhh, remember, I can't help you.

Sure, dinner might be Lucky Charms served with a side of
string cheese and a pile of goldfish, but who gives an F? You
won't have to lift a finger and they'll be busy for a long time. Or
your house will burn down. Minor inconvenience.

8. A coin hunt
This one is soooo simple. Get a fistful of coins and hide them
all over the house. Oh, kiddos, anyone want to go on a treasure
hunt?!!!! Hint, make sure you count how many coins you hide so
they'll know when to stop looking. Or don't. If they keep looking for hours, that works too.

9. A crapload of other things
Build a tent, put on a play, draw a self-portrait, set up a spa for
your stuffies, take a bath with glowsticks, make a chalk obstacle
course, write a song, make a video, ask Alexa to tell you jokes,
build a dog out of LEGOs, make a school for your dolls, give me
a back massage, etc. etc. etc.

10. Tell them to clean their room
They won't really clean it. But they also won't come back to you
for hours.

Yesterday I walked into Zoey's room and lo and behold, in front of me was the most amazing sculpture I've ever seen. Just look at how creative she is! She's the next Picasso, the next Rembrandt, the next — nahhhhh, that's bullshit.

> ME: ZOEEEEYYYYY! I am NOT buying any more
> hangers. Pick up all the clothes you threw on the floor
> and hang them back up NOW!

- - - - - - - - -

IS THIS A GOOD PINTEREST PROJECT OR A BAD PINTEREST PROJECT?

KIDS: Mommmm, can we do this art project?!

YOUR FIRST THOUGHT: Awwwww shit.

YOUR SECOND THOUGHT: I know I'm supposed to encourage their creative spirit but remember the last time?

YOUR THIRD THOUGHT: F.U. Pinterest and your stupid art projects that fool me into thinking they're gonna be easy and turn out looking beautiful.

Stay calm, use your brain, and remember this.

What Pinterest shows you:

The *finished* product, and whoever did the project probably did it 24 times and just shared a picture of the *best* version.

What Pinterest doesn't show you:

The blood, sweat, tears, yelling, cursing, whining, glitter disasters, burned fingers, dyed fingers, dyed countertops, crying mommies, crying douchenuggets, and alllllll the other levels of hell that you go through to get to that finished product.

If only there were some kind of magic guide to help you pick an art project that's not gonna make you regret ever living. A guide? Hmmmm, yes, A GUIDE!! So yup, you should absolutely feed your children's creativity and do amazing art projects with them, but BEFORE you pick some fantabulous art project, ask yourself these questions.

- Will you have to fork over a shit-ton of money at the art supply store so you won't be able to give up in the middle of the project if it sucks?
- Will you end up yelling at your kids every time they want to do part of the project because A) You don't want them to F it up, B) You don't want the project to look like crap, or C) There are dangerous things like X-Acto knives that can slice off small pinkies and hot glue guns that can scar them for life?
- Are you the kind of person who can handle the final project looking like shit because you let your kiddo do most of the work? If not, double the supplies and let them do one and you do one.
- Did you say "no" to every project your kid wanted to do and now you're picking one that YOU think looks good and you're forcing your kid to make some F'ing turkey out of doilies and they're gonna quit and you're gonna end up doing it all alone?
- Are you in way over your head and will the finished product look like you put some peanut butter on a spoon and swirled it around in the garbage can?
- Does this project contain the herpes of the art world (glitter!!) that will be all over your house for the rest of time? If it does, F to the hell no.
- When you're done with the project is it going to take up a crapload of counter space and are you gonna wonder where the F do we put this thing but your kids insist that you keep it until they haven't mentioned it in 47 days so when they're at school you throw it out and that's the day they come home and want to see their art project and freak out because it's gone?

- Will it dye your table colors or your patio colors or your skin colors so you look like you have some weird skin disease for the next three weeks during which time you will most certainly have an interview or a wedding or family pictures?
- Are you aiming higher than your skill level and is this a project only Martha Stewart can do because I know that cutting Oreos in half to make Halloween bat cupcakes seems easy, until you realize that cutting Oreos in half is F'ing impossible because they break and now you've just eaten a shitload of broken cookies and all your bats look like rats because they don't have wings?
- Will you end up doing the project alone because your kids got bored or yelled at or hospitalized or in another room watching TV or Super-Glued to the table and you just need to finish the project before it dries and then you can YouTube how to unstick them?
- Are you better off just skipping the whole stupid art project and spending some quality time together doing something less messy, less frustrating, less expensive, less scarring, and more bonding, and not in a "Super-Glued to the table" kinda way?

HOLDEN: I spy with my little eye somethinggggg green.
ME: The grass.
HOLDEN: No.
ZOEY: That sign.
HOLDEN: No.
HUBBY: My hat.

HOLDEN: No.
ZOEY: The stripe on your shorts.
HOLDEN: No.
ME: That car.
HOLDEN: No.
(this goes on for approximately 200 more guesses)
ME: We give up.
HOLDEN: The picture of the broccoli on that truck.
ME: What truck?
HOLDEN: You know, the one we saw.
ME: Like four miles ago?!!

I meannnnnnn.

ONE LAST THING:
HAVING A CREATIVE KID
KEEPS YOU ON YOUR TOES

I was downstairs in the kitchen having the most amazing peaceful hour ever when something dawned on me. Why is it so peaceful? Peace and quiet is awesome when the kids are at school or Grandma's house, but peace and quiet is NOT awesome when the kids are home and there aren't any noises coming from anywhere. Silence is not golden when you have kids. It's doo-doo brown and lipstick red and Sharpie black and other scary colors. So I went to check. Nothing in the playroom, nothing in the living room. Last but not least, I opened Holden's door.

WTF?

He was literally wrapping his entire room in a whole roll of yarn around every single piece of furniture. Hmm, that's interesting, I didn't know I was raising an F'ing spider. So you know what I said?

ME: Just clean it up when you're done. And don't eat any
    insects.

And I shut the door. Because I'm used to this stuff. I'm used
to finding the entire tape dispenser wrapped in tape.

I'm used to finding art supplies ALL over the house.

I'm used to seeing all the girls walk to school wearing pink and purple sparkly backpacks, except mine.

My kids march to the beat of a different drum. In fact, it's probably not even a drum. It's probably more like a lute or a glockenspiel. Bottom line, I just pray that people don't ostracize them for being weird. That they see them as unique, bold, out-of-the-box thinkers, builders, trendsetters, the complete opposite of boring. And that's why even though having creative kids can be a little more unpredictable and crazy and messy, I support their creativity every day. By keeping their art closet stocked, their costume bins stuffed, and their dresser drawers filled with the clothes THEY want to wear.

ME: Aggghhh, it's so windy!! My dress won't stop
    blowing up.
HOLDEN: Just tuck it in your vagina.

———°———

CHAPTER 4

If They Say "I Hate You," Then You're Probably Doing It Right

"ONE . . . TWO . . . TWO AND A HALF . . . two and three-quarters" . . . I'm using every fraction in the world so I don't have to say it . . . "two and seven-eighths" . . . don't make me say it . . . "annnnnd THREE." Awwww shit, now I gotta turn into Cujo. You'd think my rugrats would have learned by now that the second I start counting to three, they need to immediately stop whatever they're doing, whether it's reenacting WWE at the top of a tall flight of stairs, or trying to overflow their milk cups by blowing bubbles in them, or putting their tongues on the escalator handle, or trying to put a light saber up my butt while I'm washing the dishes, etc. etc. etc. But nope, they keep acting like douchenuggets.

I say, "Knock it off or I'll punish you," which totally sucks because punishing your kids is not fun. Not fun at all. They hate you for it and it makes you feel totally guilty, even though really it's the right thing to do. Because if your kid misbehaves, I feel sorry for you. But if your kid misbehaves and you don't do jack shit to stop it, I don't feel sorry for you at all. I mean, sure, at that moment your kids might love you more for being Mrs. McNiceypants and giving them a million cake pops or letting them keep their iPads, but in the end, if you don't discipline them, they'll be collect-calling you to say, "Yo, Mom, you need to come post bail. And wash my orange jumpsuit, biatch."

DEAR STRANGER WHO DISCIPLINED MY KIDDO AT THE PLAYGROUND TODAY

Dear stranger who disciplined my kiddo at the playground today,

Whoa, whoa, whoa, lemme get this straight. So today your daughter was trying to do the monkey bars? Okay, got it. And my kid was trying to do the monkey bars too? Simple enough. But since your kiddo is new to the monkey bars and takes forever and sometimes gets scared and stops right in the middle, my son had no choice but to go past her and sometimes bump her a little and she would fall and be all sensitive and start crying? Hmmm. All righty then.

Now before I continue, I just want to say that yes, I know I should have been there when this all went down, but unfortunately I was on the other side of the playground with my son's friend who was crying. So no, I wasn't there, but does that give you a right to discipline my kiddo? Does that give you the right to talk to him sternly and tell him to knock it off? Does that give you the right to act like you are the person in charge when he is actually MY child?

Ummmm, yes. YES IT DOES.

I didn't get the chance to say this today, but THANK YOU. Because if my kid is acting like a douchenugget and I'm not around for whatever reason, you have my permission to tell him to knock that shit off. I'm not saying you have the right to touch him in any way or yell at him uncontrollably (only I'm allowed to do that), but please feel free to tell him to stop being a jerkwad if he's not waiting his turn to do the monkey bars. Or if he's walking up the slide. Or if he's throwing wood chips. Or if he's saying bad words. Or being a bully. Or doing anything he shouldn't be doing that's bothering someone else.

Because even if you aren't his parent, you are the adult. Which means you are smarter than he is. And yeah, I know there are probably a-holes out there who would be all pissy about some stranger getting mad at their kiddo, but not me.

It takes a village. And these days our village might be a little bigger and more spread out and we don't all sleep in side-by-side huts or ride in covered wagons or gather around the campfire at night and we don't even all know each other, but we can either choose to have a village or not. And I choose to have a village.

I'm sorry I wasn't there to do my job, so thank you for helping me do it.

Sincerely,
"That" kid's mom

HOLDEN: Mom, can I have a snack?
ME: I'm washing dishes right now, buddy.
(five seconds later)
HOLDEN: Now can I have a snack?
ME: Still washing dishes.
HOLDEN: Now can I?
ME: Holden, do you hear the sink running?
HOLDEN: Yes. But can I have a snack?
ME: Grrrrr, after I wash the dishes!!!!!
HOLDEN: Mom?
ME: Don't you dare ask me for a snack.
HOLDEN: I'm not, I'm asking you something else.
ME: What?
HOLDEN: Are you done washing the dishes?

IF YOUR KID DROPS HIS CAKE POP ON THE
GROUND, DO YOU:

A. Buy him a new one

B. Brush it off and hand it to him

C. Keep chatting with your friend and ignore your kid who's
   screaming at the top of his lungs until the barista gives
   him a new cake pop

D. Pick it up and throw it in the trash and tell your kid,
   "Maybe next time you'll be more careful"

CORRECT ANSWER: NO F'ING IDEA.

TEN CREATIVE WAYS TO PUNISH YOUR DOUCHENUGGETS THAT MIGHT EVEN HELP YOU A LITTLE

1. Take away something you wanted to get rid of anyway

"Young lady, you are totally losing something for acting like that.
Give me that container of glitter slime right now. It's gone."

2. Make them do something that helps you out

"Your behavior is unacceptable. You'll be spending the rest of the
night sorting and folding laundry!" Muahahahahaaa.

3. Take something away you weren't
gonna give them in the first place
"That's it! We are no longer going to the Jellybean Factory!!!!"

RUGRAT: But that's not fair. I didn't know we were going to the Jellybean Factory!!

"We were and it was gonna be lots of fun."

4. Make them pay you
for their bad behavior
"Didn't I tell you to clean up the playroom? That's it, you owe me a piece of your Halloween candy for every LEGO you didn't clean up." Nom nom nom.

5. Force them to do something
that'll keep them busy for a while
"And while you're busy writing me that three-page apology note, I'll be upstairs taking a bubble bath and reading *People* magazine cover to cover."

6. Keep siblings separated
"If you two can't get along, you are no longer allowed to talk to each other."

Of course, they'll purposely get along now just to defy you.

7. Make them listen to your music as a punishment

"You guys have driven me crazy for the last time. Say adios to Kidz Bop. For the rest of the day, *I* get to pick the radio station."

8. Cancel a playdate you were dreading anyway

"Don't you talk back to me. That's it, I'm calling Dennis's mom right now and telling her he can't come over ~~today~~ ~~this week~~ this month."

9. Get a little extra cash

"The next person who leaves a light on in the house owes me a dollar. Two lights, two dollars. A light that I turned off ten minutes ago and you turned back on, enough money for me to buy those earrings I saw at Anthropologie!"

10. Find a little peace and quiet

"I've told you four times now to stop interrupting me. You have lost the right to speak for the next hour."

DOUCHENUGGET: Bu-
ME: I'm serious, not a peep.

We were having one of "those" mornings. First, Holden freaked out because Zoey used the last of the milk and she wouldn't go to the downstairs fridge to get more. I was in the bathroom and he just sat next to the door whining and complaining and I was like, dude, you have spent way more energy complaining than it would have taken to just go get another carton. Aargggh, just go get the milk!! But nope, he refused. And then when he walked away from the bathroom because I wouldn't help, he stubbed his toe and freaked out more. And then when he finally got the milk, he spilled it while he was pouring it. He was a WRECK. So finally I said, buddy, do you want to start this day over and just make it better? He said yes, so I drew a reset button on this sheet of paper.

ME: Press this reset button.
HOLDEN: That's a circle.

So I drew it better.

ME: Now push it.

He looked a little skeptical but he "pushed" it. And I acted like it worked. I climbed back into bed and pretended like I was waking up again, and he took off all his fresh clothes (even though I kept insisting this step wasn't necessary) and climbed back in his own bed and rolled out again, and both of us restarted our day. Was it flawless? Not at all. Was he a little late to school because it took a few extra minutes? Yup. But it was a helluva lot better than it was before we pushed the reset button.

ZOEY: Mom, you are the nicest mom in the whole world —

ME: Awww, thank you, Zoey.

ZOEY: — except for Charlotte's mom. She's the NICEST.

ME: Wait, what?!!

ZOEY: No, Mom, that's a good thing. You are literally the
SECOND nicest mom in the WHOLE entire world.

ME: Zoey, lemme ask you something.

ZOEY: What?

ME: Just yesterday you were saying how Charlotte was
being pretty mean to the kids at school.

ZOEY: Yeah, but her mom is REALLLLLY nice.

ME: Is it possible that her mom is TOO nice to her? Like
she lets her do whatever she wants and maybe that's why
Charlotte's not a very nice girl?

ZOEY: Ohhhhh, I never thought of that! Okay, then you
should be glad you're mean sometimes.

ME: Thanks, Zoey. Thanks a lot.

- - - - - - - - -

WHY YELLING AT YOUR KIDS MIGHT BE A GOOD THING

I was recently skimming social media (apparently I felt like squashing my self-esteem and making myself feel like every other person on earth is happier than I am) when I stumbled upon a post from an old friend. I'm pretty sure we were friends back in high school because a lot of things weren't invented yet. Shit like yoga and kale and essential oils. But then she migrated to things like Diva cups and tea tree oil and I stuck to the same stuff I liked in high school — McDonald's, chocolate, and Slurpees — so we drifted apart. Anyways, she put up a post that said something like (and I'm paraphrasing but less than you think) . . .

> SAFFRON (not her real name but it should be): You know what I hate? When I hear a mom complain that she feels guilty about yelling at her kids. Of course you feel guilty. Why would you ever yell at children? I don't understand why other moms can't make a pledge never to yell at their precious little love muffins. That's what I did.

Well, Saffron, I'll give you two reasons:

1. Kids *purposely* drive their parents to the brink of insanity.
2. Yelling at your kids sometimes can actually be a good thing. That's right, GOOD.

Because yelling once in a while (I purposely made that vague because for some moms that's twice a week and for other moms that's 497 times before breakfast) can accomplish a lot.

For example, my kids know I mean business when I yell and there's no room for misinterpretation. The moment I start sounding like the Tasmanian Devil with a bullhorn, they know that they better put their shoes on pronto or there are gonna be some serious repercussions. I mean, sure, I could just bring my voice down to a threatening whisper like Little Miss Perfect-pants does. I could also eat chia seeds and say "namaste" to the cashier at Target, but you don't see me doing that, do you?

And here's another reason moms who yell are awesome. We are people who like to show our emotions BIG TIME. This means that sometimes I yell so loud the kids down the street put on their shoes, but it also means that sometimes I say "I love you" and kiss and hug my rugrats so tight that they struggle to escape my grip. Yup, my highs are high and my lows are low, but they're also followed by yummy chocolate binges (hashtag #worthit).

Oh, and I almost forgot another benefit. Wanna know why my kiddos are besties? Because nothing makes people bond more than a common enemy. Seriously, I yell at Holden and Zoey gets all protective. I yell at Zoey and Holden backs her up. I yell at both of them and they huddle together like those adorable penguins you see in a blizzard trying to keep each other warm. Bonding—reason numero quatro.

Okay, let's move on to numero fiveo. Yelling lets my kids know I'm human. That's right, Mommy makes mistakes sometimes. Like that time I stupidly forgot to shave my bikini area before I took the kids swimming so I had to swim in shorts so no one would think two rodents had gotten into the pool. But I digress. Anyways, eventually your kids are going to figure out you're a human who makes mistakes, and it's gonna be a helluva lot less disappointing if it happens now, long before they're teenagers and already hate you.

And last but not least, yelling gives me a chance to apologize. I'm sure Saffron's like, "But, but, but if you didn't yell in the first place, you wouldn't need to apologize." Yup, I guess that's true. (I'm like the Curious George of moms. I screw up and then take credit when I apologize.) But here's the thing: If you never do anything wrong, how do you set a good example by saying you're sorry? *I* do like a million things wrong every day, but what do *you* have to apologize for, Saffron? I guess YOU could apologize for only letting them have wooden toys, or for depriving them of the joy of McDonald's french fries, or for never letting them have screen time so they turn into weirdos who think YouTube is the devil.

Anyways, my point is this. Moms shouldn't feel bad for being yellers. Because when your kid spills an entire bowl of salsa in your purse, you're allowed to yell. Or when your rugrat tries to flush a baseball down the toilet, you're allowed to yell. Or when your douchenugget takes a Sharpie to your new leather couch, you're allowed to yell. You're also allowed to take a box of Twinkies to the bathroom, lock the door, and shove all that creamy deliciousness into your pie hole and chase it with a bottle of vino until you start to feel better. Bwahahahaha, I think I just heard my old tea tree oil friend audibly gasp.

SEVEN RANDOM TIPS
TO REMEMBER WHEN YOU'RE
MAD AT YOUR KIDS

1. Never brush your daughter's hair when you're angry with her about something.
2. Try not to give out punishments that are gonna punish you, too, like taking away screen time.
3. There are two levels of taking away ice cream.
   A) When they're so naughty they lose ice cream.
   Or B) When they're soooo naughty they lose ice cream but you still get it for yourself and eat it in front of them.
4. When you're about to go ballistic on your kids, tell them you're about to go ballistic on them. It'll teach them a new vocabulary word, it'll give them one last chance, and you won't feel quite as bad when you actually go ballistic.
5. Sending them to bed early sounds like a great punishment . . . until they wake up before the ass-crack of dawn the next day.
6. When you can't think up a good punishment on the spot, feel free to say things like "or else" or "you don't want to find out" or "I promise you'll be sorry."
7. Sometimes the whisper Cujo voice is way more effective than actually yelling. Bonus: the neighbors won't call social services on you.

- - - - - - - - -

HOLDEN: (squinting) Mom, are my eyes open or closed?
ME: Ummm, open.
HOLDEN: No, they're closed. Now are they open or closed?
ME: Closed.
HOLDEN: No, they're open. Now are they open or closed?
ME: Holden, I'm done playing this game.
HOLDEN: Open or closed?
ME: I'm done playing.
HOLDEN: Just guess!!! Open or closed? Open
    or closed?!!! MOM, ARE THEY OPEN OR
    CLOSED?!!!!!!

Whoopsie, I guess they're closed since he didn't even notice
I walked away.

- - - - - - - - -

ADVICE TO MYSELF
WHEN I FEEL LIKE
I'M A SHITTY PARENT

Do you ever feel like you're a bad mom? Not like one of those cool bad moms in that movie where they look ahhhmazing in pajama pants and get wasted all the time. Like you really don't know WTF you're doing. Me too. All the time. But then I remember, I'm not a bad mom. I'm a bad dresser, a bad Pinterest-doer, a bad Girl Scout leader, a bad lunch packer, and a bad baker, but not a bad mom. So I wrote myself a list of reminders to read the next time I'm feeling like I suck at this job. Of course I probably won't be able to find it underneath all the piles of crap on my counters, so I'm putting it here in this book so I always know where it is. Feel free to borrow it if you ever need to.

1. There will always be people who judge you. People who judge you for wearing a shirt with coffee stains or walking to the mailbox without a bra on. People who back away when they see how dirty your car is. People who think you're a shitty parent because you let your kiddo wear underwear as a hat to the grocery store. Etc. etc. etc. But here's what you have to remember. You're not the jerkwad. They are, for judging. There's only one person who should be feeling bad here, and it's not you.

2. An expert might know every single little thing about their area of expertise, but there is something they will never know as well as you do. Your own child. What will help

them, what will hurt them, and what will motivate them. It's good to listen to the experts, but you don't *have to* take their advice. They might know *more* than you. But no one knows *better* than you.

3. If you're worried you're not doing a good enough job, that MEANS you're a good parent. Bad parents don't worry. Good parents worry because they care.

4. Trust your gut. If your brain is telling you something and your mom is telling you something else and your mother-in-law is telling you something different and the articles on the Internet are telling you all sorts of different things, stop listening to everyone else and go with your gut. Because if that many people think they have the right answer, there probably isn't a *right* answer. There are just lots of answers and you need to pick the one that seems right for you.

5. Everything seems worse at 2 am, so stop stressing out about problems in the middle of the night. You basically have two choices. Lie there awake worrying about it and be exhausted out of your mind tomorrow so you can't even function. Or count sheep, go to sleep, and wake up ready to face the problem head-on. With coffee. And maybe a little something in your coffee.

6. Focus on your own kid, not someone else's. There's always gonna be some shithead you want to fix. Or knock out. But that's the thing — there's ALWAYS gonna be some shithead. So you're better off teaching your kid how to deal with the shitheads, in case you're not there to eliminate them.

7. Sometimes *not* doing something for your child is actually doing the most for them. It might feel like you're being lazy or slacking off or being mean, but it's not. It's making sure they know how to do it later on when you're not there.

8. If someone gives you unsolicited advice about how to buckle your kids' car seats or get them to eat veggies or sleep through the night, and they do it in a way that makes you feel like crap, like they're judging you for doing it wrong, try not to let it get to you. Listen to their advice in case they know what they're talking about, but as soon as they're not looking, feel free to roll your eyes. Their advice might be good even if their delivery sucks. And you don't need to waste your energy or good mood on some asshat who doesn't know how to say things nicely.

9. Even when you see the worst in yourself, your kiddo is going to see the best. Like you'll remember the fourteen times you turned into a Tasmanian Devil that day, but when you're tucking them into bed, they'll still say you're the best mom in the universe. I don't know why it works this way, but it does. Thank God.

10. Being a parent is the hardest job in the world. So that means you are *literally* doing the hardest thing on earth. Like if you go to med school you can totally quit if you want. But once you have a baby, you can't give up. No matter how hard it gets, you have to keep going, and going, and going. And not just for years. For the rest of your life. So don't be too hard on yourself. Or you'll never make it.

HOLDEN: Mom, can I put cookies in Zoey's lunchbox?

ME: Awww, of course, buddy, but you better write a note so she knows it's from you and not me.

HOLDEN: She'll know. You never put cookies in. That's why she asked me to.

- - - - - - - - -

ME: Zoey, go brush your teeth.

ZOEY: I did.

ME: There is no way you did it that quickly.

ZOEY: I did! Feel my toothbrush.

ME: I didn't ask if you wet your toothbrush. I asked if you brushed your teeth.

ZOEY: I did.

ME: As in you put toothpaste on the toothbrush and brushed your teeth for two whole minutes?

ZOEY: Yes.

ME: In the amount of time it took to have this conversation, you could have just gone upstairs and brushed them.

ZOEY: Mommmm. Why would I brush my teeth AGAIN?

ME: Because you never brushed them.

ZOEY: I did. Feel my toothbrush. See, it's wet.

- - - - - - - - -

NO SHIT SHERLOCK PARENTING

You've heard of all the different kinds of parenting, I'm sure. Tiger Moms, Helicopter Parents, Attachment Parenting, Laid-Back-Go-Walk-In-The-Street Parenting (I know there's a real name for this one but I'm blanking on it), etc. Well, I'd like to add my style to the bunch. I call it No Shit Sherlock Parenting. Like here are some examples of No Shit Sherlock Parenting.

"I let my kid call all the shots around the house and now he's turned into a dickwad and freaks out whenever my hubby or I says no to something."

No Shit Sherlock.

"I desperately want to be the best mom on earth so I literally drop whatever I'm doing to cater to my cherub's every need and now she can't do anything on her own."

No Shit Sherlock.

"I've never let my child watch TV or eat McDonald's and now that he's older, he's binge-eating Taco Bell and chasing it with shot glasses of 409."

No Shit Sherlock.

I know those are all a little extreme but the truth is I see examples of No Shit Sherlock Parenting every day. Which is interesting because I think most parents pretty much know what we're SUPPOSED to do in most situations. Like if I take my kid to the grocery store and I won't buy him Sugary Boogery O's and he glues himself to the linoleum hoping I'll cave in and buy them for him, I know what I *should* do. NOT buy them. I mean, no shit Sherlock, if he throws a tantrum and gets what he wants, what's he gonna do next time? Duhhhh, throw a tantrum again.

Of course, every once in a while I say screw it and I toss a box of Sugary Boogery O's in the shopping cart to get him to shut up. Maybe I'm in a hurry to get to carpool, or I'm just not up for the fight, or my kiddo's having a rough day and could use a win. Do I know it's the wrong thing to do? No shit Sherlock. But I figure it's okay to slack off once in a while. Everything in moderation (except donut holes). And as long as I *mostly* apply No Shit Sherlock Parenting to the majority of my life, I'll end up doing an okay job.

Like if my douchenuggets aren't listening and won't put their shoes on when it's time to leave, I know what I'm supposed to do. Speak with a super firm "don't-F-with-me" voice and tell them the car is pulling out of the driveway in 90 seconds and sometimes even back the car out a few feet if they're not ready on time to show them I mean business. Do I do this every time? Nope. Sometimes I freak out and yell at them and escalate the whole situation and then feel like a total mean mommy for the rest of the day, but if I stop and take a deep breath and think about the answer, I know what I should do. Because duhhh, no shit Sherlock.

I mean, don't get me wrong, there are plenty of problems that pop up that aren't so simple to solve with No Shit Sherlock Parenting because they're a little more complicated, especially as my kiddos get older. Like when there's a relentless bully at school, or my kid sees a used condom on the street and asks what it is, or I forget about my daughter's best friend's birthday party and don't remember until ten minutes after it ended. And No Shit Sherlock Parenting might be different for different kids. Like if your kiddo has special needs, your No Shit Sherlock answers might be a little different than mine. But in most situations, if we listen to our guts, we can figure out the No Shit Sherlock answer. And if we manage to apply No Shit Sherlock Parenting to our kiddos like 80 or 90 percent of the time, we're gonna do a decent job. And that's pretty awesome considering it is literally the hardest job on earth.

ME: Let's go potty.
ZOEY: But I don't have to.
ME: Just try.
ZOEY: Fiiiine.

We walk into separate stalls. I hear her lock the door, pull off some toilet paper, flush, and come out.

ZOEY: Okay, I tried.
ME: Seriously, Zoey?
ZOEY: Yes!
ME: You forgot to do something.
ZOEY: What?
ME: Turn around. You were facing the toilet the whole time.
ZOEY: (blank stare)
ME: Go back in and really try.
ZOEY: Fiiiine.

TIP: When I have a problem and don't know what to do, I like to pretend it's actually my friend who has the problem and picture her telling me about it, and then I picture what advice I would give her, and then I usually have my answer.

Dear everyone sitting near us on the airplane,

I would like to apologize to you because my son is going to be a d-bag for the first 20 minutes of our flight. Then it will get better. You see, at the beginning of our vacation, I told him, "I need you to behave. And every time you don't behave, it's ten minutes off your iPad time on the airplane." Well, he lost 20 minutes. And I can either follow through with the punishment and he'll be a d-bag for the first 20 minutes of the flight, or I can just let him play his iPad, but then he'll be a d-bag for the rest of his life. So 20 minutes it is. I'm so sorry! But a mom's gotta do what a mom's gotta do.

Sincerely,
The woman in 17C who is literally
counting down the minutes

ONE LAST THING: SOMETIMES BEING A GOOD MOM FEELS LIKE BEING A TOTAL BITCH

Do you know how much it sucks constantly correcting and scolding your kid? You feel like you're the meanest mommy on earth, like you're this total nag who can't stop telling them what to do. Clean up your plate, say please, stop interrupting me, put your laundry in your hamper, do not hit your brother, do not lick your sister, I didn't hear you say thank you, I better not get a phone call, I said no, what part of no are you not understanding, knock it off, etc. etc. etc. But here's the thing. Every time you correct your kiddo, you're helping steer them back to the right path. See?

x

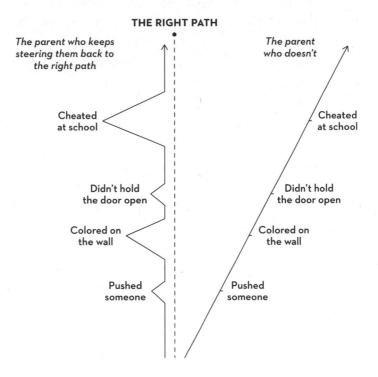

And do you see what happens to the kiddo whose parents don't constantly steer them back? They get farther and farther and farther away from the right path, and pretty soon they're like 9 miles away from it and the kid's doing drugs and dealing drugs and dropping out of school and holding up the 7-Eleven and they're featured in the local newspaper blotter and their parents are like awwwww shit, whatta we do now? And they throw up their hands or have to pay a crapload for professional help because the distance between the right path and the wrong path seems too daunting and too late.

Stop reading. That's right, stop reading right now and I want you to sit there and think. Do you know any parents like this? Ones who let their douchenuggets constantly get away with shit? Maybe it's that person you used to be friends with. Or maybe it's that person you're still friends with but now you can only go out with the parents because every time you let your kids hang out with their kids, one of your kids ends up in a headlock being forced to eat the carpet. Or maybe you ARE those parents.

In which case I am NOT telling you it's hopeless. Not at all. In fact, I'm telling you to take action now because the longer you wait, the farther that line gets from the right path and the harder it gets to steer them back, so start correcting it now.

But anyways, I forgot where I was going with this. Oh yeah, I'm a mean mommy. But there's a reason I'm a mean mommy. There's a reason I scold, punish, yell, remind, and take desserts away over and over and over again. To keep my kids on the right path. And one day they're gonna thank me for it. Or not. Probably not. But at least they won't be "not thanking me" from the penitentiary. And even if they are in the pen, at least they'll be saying please and thank you to the cafeteria lady when she spoons gray mashed potatoes onto their tray.

\- - - - - - - - -

(7:58am)

For some reason I thought it would be a fun experiment to count how many times I say "no" to my kids in a day. I lost count at 7:58 am.

CHAPTER 5

———o———

Write "Have Fun" on a Sticky Note So You Won't Forget

I KNOW WHAT YOU'RE PROBABLY thinking after reading that last section. That I'm a total bitch. Well I'm not a *TOTAL* bitch. A partial one sometimes and a total one other times, but if you averaged out all of my days and made a graph of how bitchy I am, this is where I'd probably fall:

One of those super sweet moms who makes Pinterest projects and never yells ●————————————● Me ————————————● Total bitch

Being a good parent is a balancing act. There are days you're gonna be alllllllllllll the way over on the right side of that line (maybe even off the page) and there are days you're gonna be allllllllll the way over on the left side up to your elbows in F'ing glitter because your kiddo wanted to do some stoopid art project (and you said yes) and halfway through it you're gonna be like WTF was I thinking. But now it's too late to quit and your douchenuggets are off in another room playing on their iPads while you curse the fact that you just spent $500 at Michaels to torture yourself while you spend some quality time with your kiddos. Not. But I digress.

Anyways, here's the thing. It's okay to freak out and yell at your kids when you tell them to get their shoes on and they decide that's the moment they need to poop their brains out so you're twenty minutes late to school, as long as you balance it out with amazing, awesome, fun moments they will remember forever and ever and that will overshadow all the times you accidentally turned into Hannibal Lecter. Whoopsies.

This is that section. The section where I look like a mom who's super nice and totally fun. So if you've been reading this book straight through, you're gonna think, okay, she's actually not a total bitch. But if anyone happens to open this book to this section and didn't read this book in chronological (you have NO idea how many times I just had to type that word to spell it right) order, they're gonna think I'm the most awesome mom on earth. Muahahahahahaaaaa, joke's on them.

FUN IS...

Fun is farting as loud as you can right before you say good night and close your kiddo's bedroom door.

Fun is calling each other by your names spelled backwards all day.

Fun is having breakfast for dinner, breakfast for lunch, and breakfast for breakfast because breakfast is the best meal and upside-down day doesn't work because no one wants to eat chicken and broccoli for breakfast.

Fun is taping up pictures of monkeys in every cabinet and drawer all over the house when you're leaving on a business trip so your family finds them after you're gone.

Fun is giving your kid a bowl of ice cream in the bathtub (fun for you too because you won't worry about the mess).

Fun is bringing your kids to school on a Sunday because it's April Fools' Day.

Fun is going to the movies dressed up in costumes that go with the movie.

Fun is getting onto the ice skating rink with your kids even if you suck because they love when they're better than you at something.

Fun is letting your kid help you pump the gas because it makes them feel more grown up.

Fun is lining your whole family up at one end of the living room and having tushie races to see who can scoot to the other side first without using their hands.

Fun is going into another room when your kids want to pop bubble wrap and it's driving you insane but you don't want to stop them from having fun.

Fun is having a burping contest even though you know it's totally the wrong thing to teach your kids.

Fun is taking your kiddo to Sephora and saying let's go crazy.

Fun is getting in the pool with your kids and not being the mom who sits on the lounge chair because you just blow-dried (blew dry???) your hair even though sometimes I'm that mom but every time I get in the pool I realize it's way more fun and totally worth messing up my hair.

Fun is piling all the warm laundry that just came out of the dryer on top of your kiddo on a cold day.

Fun is writing your kid a letter from their balloon that flew away and telling them what a wonderful adventure Mr. Balloon is having out in the world.

Fun is making a ~~schmorgusborg~~ ~~schmorgasburg~~ schmorgasborg (WTF, I have no idea how to spell that word) for dinner of easy crap like chicken nuggets and cheese and crackers and sliced-up hot dog and giving your kids little toothpicks to eat it with.

Fun is making tiny drops of pancake batter while you're cooking pancakes so you can serve your kids a stack of baby pancakes.

Fun is letting go of the stress and the anxiety and the laundry and the dishes and the homework and the cooking and the chores and the responsibilities and knowing it's not gonna kill you to do it all tomorrow and just have fun with your family today.

ZOEY: Mom, look how pretty the clouds are today. Can we
    take a picture of them?
ME: Sure.

So I pulled the car to the side of the road and we took this.
And right after we finished, it broke apart and looked totally different. I'm always rushing around trying to get the kids places,
but every once in a while I remember to slow down to appreciate
the moment. I'm going to try to do this more often.

(Holden blows his nose)
(I purposely fart at the same time)
ME: Holden, your nose sounds like a toot!
(He blows his nose again)

(I fart at the same time)

ME: OMG, Holden, that's amazing.

(He is dyyyying of laughter and blows his nose again)

(I try but nothing comes out this time)

HOLDEN: Oh no, my nose is broken.

ME: Try again.

(He blows his nose)

(I manage to squeeze a little one out)

HOLDEN: Bwahahahahahahahahaha.

ME: See, not broken.

HOLDEN: I wish it were broken, it reeks in here. I better
stop doing that.

CAN YOU GO TO HELL
FOR TELLING THE
TOOTH FAIRY TO F OFF?

Dear Tooth Fairy,

You suck. Yup, I said that. You act like you're just this
sweet little innocent pixie with wings who brings joy and
happiness to all the little girls and boys across the land,
but at whose expense? OURS. The parents.

I mean, let's just start with the most obvious reason
you suck. Exhibit A: You collect teeth. Wanna know
who else in the world collects teeth? Serial killers. As
in a small handful of sickos who get their jollies from

killing human beings. Which puts you in a very exclusive group: tooth fairies and serial killers (they meet on the third Sunday of every month in a room at the YMCA and it's basically just a roomful of white guys walking around with creepy smiles as tiny sparkles zoom in and out between them).

Know what else makes you suck? When little Timmy comes running out of school wearing a humongous smile with a brand-new hole in his mouth and alllllllll evening long I'm reminding myself, "Don't forget the tooth fairy, don't forget the tooth fairy, don't forget the tooth fairy," and then I slip on my fat pants, sip a little wine, watch a little mindless TV, and go to sleep, only to bolt upright in bed at 3 am in a cold sweat because OMG, I forgot to swap out the tooth!! So I fumble around in the dark trying to find a couple of dollar bills (who the hell has cash anymore?), so I have to go to my hubby's drawer (because men always have cash for some weird reason) and sneak quietly into my kiddo's room and fetch the tooth and fold the bills like 9,000 times so I can cram them into the miniscule box and then the next morning . . .

HOLDEN: MOMMMMMM, LOOOOOOK!!!!!!!
The tooth fairy left me $200!!!!!!!

Awwww crap, I knew I should have turned on the light. Looks like we're eating mac & cheese for the rest of this month (as opposed to what we were gonna eat — mac & cheese).

Or worse, little Timmy comes pitter-pattering into my room at 5 am because "Boohoohoooo, why did the tooth fairy forget about me, Mommy?" Because she sucks, Timmy. Because she sucks. I mean, technically I know it was me who forgot, but if you didn't exist, I wouldn't have to remember yet another F'ing thing on top of alllllllllll the things I'm already responsible for.

Of course, something else wouldn't happen either if you didn't exist.

This.

This giant toothless smile because he is sooooooo-oooooo excited. Not for the money. Not because he can brag to his friends about how many teeth he's lost now. But because you visited him last night. The belief that a magical little fairy slipped into his room and wanted HIS tooth so much that she paid him for it and even left a little pixie dust behind (glitter, yet another reason I hate you) makes him giddy with happiness.

This smile is why we agree to be your accomplice. And why as much as I think you suck and rarely say your name without a few four-letter words before it, I also kind of love you. Because anyone who can make my child THIS happy can't be all bad.

Sincerely,
You owe me $200

ZOEY: Mom, how will the tooth fairy know where I am if I'm at Grandma's tonight?

ME: She'll know. She's magic!

ZOEY: Nooo, I don't think so. I'll just sleep at home.

ME: Don't be silly. We'll leave her a note!

ZOEY: No, she'll just fly away when she sees I'm not in my bed. I'll just sleep here.

After a lot of back and forth, we finally figured out a solution. We wrote a note to the tooth fairy and taped it on Zoey's window outside so she wouldn't fly away without seeing it.

Sometimes you have to go to *great* lengths to keep the magic alive. But mostly to make sure they still sleep at Grandma's.

MINIVAN DOORS
ARE SO OVERRATED

I live in a town where almost everyone drives one of three fancy cars. Don't ask me what kind of cars they are because I have no F'ing idea (except for the Teslas that are easy to spot because of their crazy door handles that I still have no idea how they work, do you push them???), but pretty much every mom drives one of three fancy cars. The reason that sentence says "pretty much every mom" and not "every mom" is because of me. I'm the one mom who doesn't drive a fancy something-or-other. I drive a shitty old minivan.

But here's the thing: I love my shitmobile. I love that it still has buttons that stick out on the radio instead of a flat screen so I can keep my eyes on the road and blindly feel for the different channels and know exactly where #3 is without looking. And I love that it has 47 cup holders, even if they're all filled with sticky shit with dirt shit stuck to the sticky shit. And I love that the side pocket of the driver's seat is filled with Bed Bath & Beyond coupons that go all the way back to 1951 because they never expire.

Yup, I love my minivan. Well, I loved it. Until this happened. I was schlepping Holden to the store because we needed sunscreen for a vacation we were going on when I suddenly realized we needed to stop at the post office so I quickly turned the corner and . . .

"Mommmmmmyyyyy, look!!!!"

"I can't look now, buddy, I'm driving."

"But Mommmmyyyyy!!!"

"I'll look at the next red light, bud."

"Mommm!!!!!!"

"Holden Luke Alpert, if I look right now, we'll get into a car accident and die. Is that what you want?!!"

"But, Mom, the door is open!"

And that's when I realize the temperature of the car does feel a bit nippy so I glance back. WTF? The minivan door is wide open and Holden is about to become a stunt double for *The Fast and the Furious*. I quickly pull over, shut it, and make sure everything is locked before we drive away again.

La la la la laaaaa, that was weird but everything's back to normal now. Until we turn the next corner and phwooop, the door slides open again.

"Mommmmmm!!!!!"

A fancy car passes us just at that moment and this Lululemony woman wearing a visor is frantically pointing to our open door to let me know about it. No shit, Sherlock. It's not like it's a busted brake light I can't see (shhh, don't tell her I didn't notice it at first). Anyways, I debate whether I should have Holden hold the door closed all the way home, or whether I should put him in a different seat. I opt for the back right seat so he's as far away from the broken door as he can be, and we manage to get home without either of us accidentally falling out. I pull the car into the garage and I get out and use all of my strength to manually close the door.

And then we walk into the house past a hole in the wall that's been there for years from God knows what. And then I go into the kitchen and I wonder what I can cook for dinner that doesn't involve the oven because our oven broke a few months ago and I haven't fixed it yet. And then I log onto my laptop that's so old it sounds like a rocket ship is taking off. And I think about alllllllll the things we need to fix/replace/patch/paint/service/duct tape around here. But I can't do any of it right now. We don't have any money left. Because tomorrow we're leaving on a HUGE vacation to Disney World and it's costing us an arm and a leg. Like an insane amount of money because we didn't want to hold back and we went all out. Reservations at an amazing hotel, Park Hopper passes to all the parks, tickets to the Happily Ever After Dessert Party, and like a million other awesome things. And I know what you're thinking. Why would you book a super expensive vacation when you need all those things fixed in your life? When you need a new car, new wall, new stove, new dishwasher, new computer, new windows, etc. etc. etc.? At the end of your seven-day vacation, aren't you going to be standing there with all of your broken stuff and the wind blowing through your minivan and think, "Awww shit, I just spent thousands of dollars and I don't have anything to show for it."

I will not. NOT. AT. ALL.

Because I WILL have something to show for it. And I'm not talking about the giant stuffed animals the kids insist on schlepping back, or the wristbands they insist on keeping, or the ears or pins or necklaces or souvenir cups or plastic figurines or tickets or other crap that manages to make it into the suitcase before I sneak them into the tiny trashcan in our hotel room that is literally so overflowing I have to stack a pile of trash next to it. That's just stuff. I'm talking about something else.

If I went out and bought a brand-new sparkly Tesla tomorrow and asked my kids in 20 years what happy memories they have from their childhood, they're not going to say the car. They're going to remember the things that happened in the car.

The talks we had. The laughter we had. The trips we took. The songs we sang at the top of our lungs. The songs I sang at the top of my lungs just to annoy them. The time I threatened to make them ride on the roof down the highway because they were annoying the crap out of me. That's what they'll remember.

Just this very moment while I was writing this story Holden came into the room and he asked what I was doing and I said I was writing about the time the minivan door slid open and he started laughing. He didn't remember that it was a shitty car that was dying a slow death because we chose a vacation instead. He was like bwahahahaha, and you made me sit in the way back!!

Don't get me wrong. If I had an unlimited amount of money (I'll find out if this is true next week when I win the lottery) I would definitely buy a Tesla. No wait, F that, I would buy a Ferrari. And I would pull up in the carpool line in my Ferrari and I'd be like F you bitches who turned up your noses at my pajama bottoms back in the day. Oh, and I would STILL be wearing pajama bottoms but no one would turn up their noses anymore because I'd be driving a badass Ferarri. Holy crap, did I just digress big time or what? Anyways, what was I saying?

Oh yeah, our most kickass family memories aren't stuff. They're experiences. Sometimes they're the small memories that made us die of laughter, like the time my rugrats were brushing their teeth and Holden spat in the sink only he didn't notice his sister's head was there and he spat on her head. And sometimes they're the memories we have to pay for. Like the time we spent nine million dollars to go to Disney World.

And since I'm writing this after the fact, I can tell you that spending nine million dollars to go to Disney was worth every penny and here's why. There was this moment when we were there and I was holding Holden and watching the fireworks from our primo lawn seats that we paid an insane amount for so we wouldn't be squished between crowds of sweaty people. And Holden's little face was smushed against mine and there were literally tears in my eyes. Not because I tear up every time I hear any Disney song. Not because the light show and fireworks were one of the coolest things I've ever seen. Because of the indelible moment I was having with my son. A moment that was gonna last in my brain and hopefully his forever and ever. It was worth a million gazillion bazillion dollars. And definitely worth driving around a few extra months with a broken shitmobile door.

IF YOU'RE PLANNING A FAMILY VACATION DO YOU:
A. Pick a time that the kids are off school
B. Pull them out of school for a few days and feel guilty about it
C. Pull them out of school and feel totally fine because the last thing you want to do is spend a crapload of money to go somewhere that's at full capacity and wait in ridiculously long lines and feel like a sardine in a swimming pool full of baby pee and have a crappy time because the whole purpose of going on a family vacation is to have a good time together

CORRECT ANSWER: I MEAN, SERIOUSLY? I THINK IT'S PRETTY OBVIOUS WHICH ONE I LEAN TO.

The most amazing thing happened. I was walking through the store with Zoey and she pointed out a shirt she wanted. It said "Smart and Beautiful Like Mom." Really?! Seriously?!! My heart just about exploded I was so happy.

ME: I wish they had a shirt like that for ME to wear.

And then I decided that was stupid. I need to stop wishing and MAKE it happen. So I went to Michaels and did.

- - - - - - - - -

THE TIME WE HOSTED
BURNING MAN AT OUR HOUSE
KINDA SORTA

F me. Yes, I know those probably aren't the classiest words to start a story with, but I really can't think of two better words to describe the shitstorm that I brought upon my house. Are you ready for this tragedy?

One Saturday night we went out with friends to a Mexican joint, and I don't know about you, but when I go to a Mexican joint, I drink. A lot. The menu said peach mango strawberry margarita, and I was like, yummmmmmmmmmm, I'll have THAT.

WAITRESS: Which one?
ME: The peach mango strawberry margarita.
WAITRESS: Which one?

Uhhhhh, WTF? There are no commas between those flavors.

ME: Oh, is that not one margarita?
WAITRESS: You want them all mixed together?
ME: F yeah.

FYI, I did not actually say the words "F yeah." What I actually said was, "Gffh bleeah," because I had just shoveled a handful of homemade tortilla chips that are clearly made with crack into my pie hole.

And then the waitress came back with my huge-ass triple fruity margarita and I sucked that bad boy down. And then after that, I had a mojito. And then we went to a bar where I drank beer and won at darts. That is not relevant to this story, but I'm just bragging.

Anyways, to make a long story short, before we went to bed that night I forgot to move our GD Elf on the Shelf. Yup, the next morning he was still sitting at the bottom of the stairs exactly where he was all day. So when Holden ran into our room begging to go search for Christmas Light (the name of our elf), I was like awwwww shit and I quickly convinced him to stay in our room for a few minutes while I raced downstairs to move him.

Shit shit shit, where can I put him quickly before Holden catches me moving him? Agggghhh, why does he have to be so floppy? Why can't he have Velcro hands so I can clip him somewhere? Oh I know, I'll put him in the oven and make him peeking out and I'll put the oven light on.

(3 MINUTES LATER)
HOLDEN: I found him!!! I found him!!!

And that's where he sat, peering out at us through that little window all day long. Until . . .

(9 HOURS LATER)
HUBBY: Want to go out for dinner?

ME: (with an eye roll because WTF? Does he think we're made of money??) No, I have chicken and broccoli to cook.

So I turned on the oven to preheat it. Our kids had some friends over and their dad had arrived to pick them up but he was sitting at our table drinking a beer because the kids didn't want to leave yet.

BEER-MOOCHING FRIEND: Karen, there's a fire in your oven.

What?!! Holy crap!!!! He's right!! And that's when I opened the door to find this gruesome scene.

Noooooooooooooooooooooooooooooooo!!!!!! All three adults crouched around the oven watching poor little Elfy burn because apparently none of us are very good at handling emergencies and we had no idea what to do.

And then suddenly the kids came in.

ME: STAY OUT OF THE KITCHEN!!!!!!! GET OUT, GET OUT!!!

I knew the kids could NOT see this. Seriously, seeing their beloved elf up in flames would scar them for life.

OBLIVIOUS CHILDREN: Why, Mommy? What's that smell?
ME: NOTHING! NOTHING!! IT'S NOT YOUR ELF BURNING. IT'S, UHHH, THE BROCCOLI. YEAH, YUP, THAT'S IT. I BURNED THE BROCCOLI.

And I slammed the kitchen door in their faces and the adults watched the rest of Christmas Light go up in flames as we heard his little elf voice screaming . . .

ELF: Hellllpppppppp meeeeee!!! It hurrrrtttts!!!

Then it was over.

And our friend used the kitchen tongs to extract the crisp limbs and head from the bottom of the oven and we put his smoking leftovers on the back porch (anyone know where I can get an itty-bitty urn??). And then twenty minutes later we were packing up to go to Noodles & Company because I decided not to cook in our oven because it was now coated in the carcinogenic remains of a melted polyester and plastic elf. But as soon as we got home, Zoey started screaming.

ZOEY: Mommmmmm!!!! Christmas Light is missing!!!!!!

Awwww shit, she noticed the empty oven.

ME: Ummmm, he told me he had to go away for a few days.
ZOEY: What?

ME: He left me a note.
ZOEY: Where?

And I ran as fast as possible upstairs and jotted out a barely legible note.

ME: (out of breath) See?

I read it out loud.
And there it was. The brokenhearted look in her eyes. Shit, I F'ed up. I had to fix this.

So three hours later, as soon as the kids were nestled all snug in their beds, I jumped on Amazon to order a new elf, only the little F'er was out of stock and wouldn't arrive for at least six days and my note said three days, so now I had to order a more expensive version that comes with a stupid scarf and booties, and he'd be here the next afternoon. Let's just pray the kids don't notice that the elf's face has been modified a little over the years and now he looks cuter. But it's okay because I've already prepared my answer.

> ME: Wow, I don't know where Christmas Light went for three days, but I'm guessing a spa vacation. He looks so well rested and revitalized!!

And now every year when I take out Christmas Light 2.0 and look at his rosy face, I remember the look of Christmas Light 1.0's face when he was going up in flames. My kids better appreciate all the shit I've done when they grow up. Because I'm pretty sure this whole experience took a few years off my life.

HOLDEN: Mom, when's my half birthday?
ME: No (F'ing) idea.
HOLDEN: We have to know so we can celebrate it.
ME: No one celebrates half birthdays, buddy.
HOLDEN: But why not?

Hmmmm, I mean, doing it once doesn't make me one of those insane Pinteresty moms, does it? JUST once. So I cut a party hat in half, bought half a cake, and hung up a banner that says "Happy Bir." I hope it is a wonderful moment that he remembers for many, many months and then forgets because there ain't no way I'm doing this every year.

- - - - - - - - -

BEING A MOM IS LIKE CONSTANTLY EATING A PLATE OF SHIT, SO DON'T FORGET TO DO THIS ONCE IN A WHILE

When you're a mom, there is constantly sooooooo much shit to do. Taking care of the house, the kids, the groceries, the carpools, your hubby, the activities, the pets, etc. etc. etc. I mean, just cleaning out the kids' closets every time they have a growth spurt (every hour on the hour) is basically a full-time job. So I don't have a to-do list. I have an "I'm lucky if I get 30 percent of this done" list. I mean, let's just take a quick look at the expression "I have a lot of shit on my plate." Guess what it implies. That you have shit to eat. So as moms, we are constantly eating shit but the shit never gets fully eaten and keeps multiplying so you always have more shit to eat. And this, my friends, is why I turn into a cranky bitch so often. Because while everyone else is sitting around watching their iPads or leaving half-finished LEGO sets on the dining room table or zoning out in front of a Sunday football game, I'm eating fecal matter.

Which is why I have to *remind* myself to have fun. I need to figure out a way to squeeze in a little joy wherever I can so my kids see me as a playful human being and not a bitchy android who just does chores and yells at them all day long. It's not about *waiting* for fun moments to pop up. It's about *making* fun moments. Because that shit ain't gonna happen unless you *make* it happen.

When Zoey and Holden were little and Zoey was in kindergarten but Holden was still in preschool, there was this weird 25-minute gap I had every morning between the time I dropped Zoey off and the absolute earliest minute I could drop Holden off. Seriously, I was ALWAYS the first person at his school drop-off before anyone else was there.

It drove me insane. All those dead minutes with nothing to do. Like I would desperately search my mind to come up with some little random errand I could shove into those 25 minutes, but honestly, how many times can one mom run to Walgreens in a single week? So we'd usually drive to school and wait in the empty parking lot reading books or watching mindless brain-sucking videos on my phone.

But then something happened. One day those dead minutes ended up being the best minutes *BECAUSE* we had nothing to do. As we were pulling into the parking lot, there was a huge puddle of water at the entrance, and as my car drove through it, it made one of those humongous waves on the sides of the car.

HOLDEN: Whoaaaa!!

And Holden thought it was the best thing on earth and couldn't stop giggling. I drove to the first parking spot like I always did, put the car into park, and Holden unbuckled to come join me in the front seat to watch some videos.

ME: Wait, I forgot something. Sorry, buddy, buckle
     back up.

So he crawled back into the back seat (I'm sure I yelled at him to stop stepping on the armrest) and I pulled out of the parking lot to the exit. And guess where I drove? Not to Walgreens or Starbucks or the grocery store. I drove about forty feet back to the entrance and through that giant puddle again. Only this time I went a little faster so the wave was even bigger and Holden was even more amazed by it. And again I pulled around and through the exit back to the entrance, even faster this time. Woooosh!!

We must have driven in and out of the school twenty times. I'm sure if anyone was in the building watching they were like WTF, but I didn't care. My son was having the best time ever watching that giant wave, and I was having the best time ever watching him in the rearview mirror. In hindsight, it was probably a really stupid thing to do to my car, but car schmar. I didn't stop until I saw other parents pulling in to drop off their kids, and only then did I pull my car around to park and walk Holden into the building. We weren't the first ones to arrive that day.

And in case you're wondering, I wasn't lying to Holden when I said I forgot something back in the parking lot. I did forget something. I forgot that I'm a mom whose whole life is about eating a never-ending pile of shit off my plate. And for fifteen minutes or so it was like I was eating a HUGE piece of glorious, fun, sweet cake. And those are the moments I ~~hope think~~ know my son will remember.

RUGRATS: Can we have dessert?

ME: Sure, tilt your heads back. (I put a cookie on each of their foreheads.) You can have dessert *if* you can get the cookies into your mouths without using your hands.

I usually make them eat their veggies to get dessert, but it's fun to change it up once in a while.

- - - - - - - - - -

The kind of parent I thought I'd be:
"Sweetie pie, make sure you're a gentleman and try to stifle your toots and belches and say excuse me if you can't."

The kind of parent I am:
It was bedtime, and when my hubby went downstairs to get Holden a little water, I was like oooooh, I've got a hilarious idea. So I crawled into Holden's bed and I buried myself behind him and all his stuffed animals.

ME: Shhhhh, don't tell Daddy I'm here.
HOLDEN: What are you doing?
ME: Shhhhhhhhhhh. Be quiet.

And then my hubby came back in the room with the water.

HUBBY: Here you go, Holden. Good ni—

And just as he was about to close the door, I let it rip. A GIANT fart. One of those loud, lonnnnng ones.

HUBBY: What was that?!! Holden!

Holden was trying to say, "It wasn't me," but he couldn't even get the words out, he was dyyying of laughter.

HUBBY: I'm not sticking around here.

And as he was closing the door again, FAAARRRRRTTT.

HUBBY: Holden!!!!
HOLDEN: It (air suck) wasn't (air suck) me
   (giggles galore).
HUBBY: Oh yeah? You're the only one in here.
   Good night.

And he quickly shut the door.
Bwahahahahahaha!! Tears were rolling down our cheeks we were laughing so hard. And I'm pretty sure Holden will remember this moment for the rest of his life. And hopefully tell his own kids about it one day. Or better yet, do the same thing to them.
I'm so glad I'm not the kind of parent I thought I'd be.

- - - - - - - - -

WHY I DON'T GO ALL OUT
(OR EVEN HALF OUT OR A QUARTER OUT)
FOR KIDS' BIRTHDAY PARTIES

FRIEND: What's the theme of Holden's birthday party?
ME: Throw a bunch of kids in the backyard.
FRIEND: (waiting with anticipation)
ME: With a sprinkler.

I mean, don't get me wrong. You wanna throw a crapload of effort and thought and money and craftiness into your kiddo's birthday party theme, all power to you. Some kids love shit like that. And some moms love to do shit like that. But not me. I learned my lesson years ago when Zoey was just one year old.

I remember the day. I was crouching down in our mudroom to pick something up off the floor when I noticed something. What's that smell? Ewwww, what is that? I leaned over to check Zoey's diaper. Nope. I looked in the bottom of the stroller to see if maybe there's a forgotten sippy cup that was once milk and is now cottage cheese. Nope. WTF is that? And that's when I realized what the smell was. Me. Ruh-rohhh, when was my last shower?

Right then and there I decided something. It was time to start being a human being again. I mean, Zoey was now over a year old and I needed to come out of this weird fog I'd been living in since the day she was born. It was time to shower at least twice a week. It was time to stop walking around the house like a topless cow with udders. And most of all, it was time to find a social life again (other than the riveting one I had at Gymboree and Kindermusik). Right then and there I decided this was going to be the year to "get out there more." So I headed to the tiny neighborhood park with Zoey. But as soon as I was within a block of the park I could see that it wasn't empty. Shit, there's someone there. Aggghhh, I don't want to chitchat with anyone. I had two choices:

A. Pretend like we're just out for a walk and skip the park and start walking home.
B. Do what I promised I was going to do. Get out there more.

Fiiine. So I turned into the park and plopped Zoey in the baby swing two swings down from the lady and her kid.

LADY: Hi.
Crap.
ME: Hi.
LADY: This is my daughter, Easton.
ME: This is Zoey.

Small talk, small talk, small talk.

ME: Well, it was nice meeting you.
WOMAN: Hey, I know we just met, but do you guys want to come to Easton's birthday party this Saturday?!
ME: Ummm, uhhhh . . .

(Get out there more, get out there more, get out
  there more.)

ME: . . . sure.

Fuck. Why did I say yes? Oh yeah, my stupid promise to get
out there more. Even if this woman seemed a little too put together for me. Even if she was wearing lip gloss and earrings in
the middle of the day. Even if I couldn't show up to the party
wearing drawstring pants carrying a four-pack of White Claw
(or whatever the popular mommy-juice was in 2010, something
between Zima and White Claw).
  Anyways, the day of the party came and I thought about bail-
ing like 60 times and kept pestering my hubby about it.

ME: Whatta you think? Should I go?
HUBBY: Go if you want to.
ME: I don't want to. But should I?
HUBBY: If you don't want to go, don't go.
ME: But maybe I should.
HUBBY: (blank stare)
ME: Fine, I'll go.

So Zoey and I jumped into the car and drove to a complete
stranger's house. I could tell which one it was from approximately four miles away. The one with the **GIANT** (seriously,
there's not a font big enough) arc of turquoise balloons stretch-
ing across the yard.

ZOEY: Ooooooh.

We walked into the backyard and I could already tell I was in WAY over my head. Holy crap, did she hire Pinterest personally to come decorate?! It was like we were actually walking into Ariel's grotto (BTW, I don't know WTF a grotto is, but that's what they call it at Disney). Everywhere I looked there were turquoise and lavender poufs tucked under tents that were covered with seaweed and decorated with sea stars and strands of faux pearls (or were they even faux?!).

And even though I actually showered that morning, and even though I had put on my fanciest sweatpants that weren't ridiculously pilled in the chub rub area, and even though I re-did my mommy bun like four times so it wasn't exploding with stray hairs, I still felt wayyyy out of place. Like I was tempted to step behind the bar and start serving the guests so that everyone could say, "Ohhh, I was wondering who that was. She's the help. Now it makes sense!"

Anyways, Zoey was struggling to get down so I plopped her on the grass and she started toddling to the nearest tent.

HOSTESS: Ahoy, new friend I met at the park!!
ME: Ahoy.

WTF, did I seriously just say that?

HOSTESS: I was just telling the girls about you! I'll
    introduce —

She literally stopped midsentence.

HOSTESS: No, no, no, sweetie, don't do that! They're not
supposed to be moved.

Zoey was stomach down on top of a pouf and was starting
to roll. Luckily the hostess didn't reach her before Zoey got dis-
tracted and abandoned the pouf to go check out the real live
mermaid across the party. I shit you not. There was a woman
wearing a mermaid tail and a clamshell bra reclining on a lounge
chair. If I wore clamshells they'd be around my waist like pasties
on the ends of long tube socks. Don't picture that.

Anyways, I was about to tell the hostess how beautiful everything looked but when I turned around, she was gone, bolting
across the yard to stop a group of kids from taking food from the
grownup snack table.

HOSTESS: No no no, kids (through a gritted-teeth smile),
those are the snacks for the grownups. Your snacks are
over there!

One table was covered with crustless sandwiches cut into sea
stars and orange and white chocolate poured into molds to look
like coral, while the other table had Goldfish crackers and little
cups of blue Jell-O with Swedish fish (probably not the kind of
Jell-O cups I'd serve at a party). And once she was done steering
them to the "right" table, she was telling another group of kids to
stay out of the toy bin, that those toys weren't for *this* party. And
so on and so on while I closely follow behind Zoey making sure
she didn't touch or play with anything that wasn't supposed to

be touched or played with, which was pretty much everything. I constantly heard the hostess saying things like, "No no no" and "Those are only for decoration" and "Please don't do that." Until finally it was time to sing Happy Birthday and everyone was instructed to gather around a highchair that was draped with a fancy birthday banner. Everyone headed over except for one person. The party girl. She was standing across the yard with a sea star in one hand and her other hand down her tights.

> HOSTESS: Easton, put down the sea star and come here, sweetie pie.
> EASTON: No.
> HOSTESS: It's time for cakie!!
> EASTON: (paraphrased) F.U.
> HOSTESS: Easton, come to Mommy!!

But apparently Easton had had enough, and it was at this moment that she pulled her hand out from inside her tights and something was in her fist. What was she holding? And then I realized. No. Nooooooo. But yup.

> HOSTESS: Easton Caroline, you put that down right now.

But it was too late. Easton was squeezing her fingers and poop was literally being squished out like Play-Doh (I'm guessing her mom never let her play with real Play-Doh and this was the closest thing maybe?) and there was a mixture of ewwwws and nervous laughter from the crowd of mommies. As entertaining as all this was, fecal matter is where I draw the line, so I grabbed Zoey. That was it. I never met "the girls," or took a picture of Zoey with the mermaid, or got any crustless sandwiches or three-tiered cake. But I'll tell you what I did get. A BIG lesson.

When it comes to birthday party themes, I can go all out and make it the most un-F'ing-believable party theme ever, and I'll be proud of it and my friends will be impressed, and I can share it on social media and get a shit-ton of likes and loves and wows, but here's the thing. Birthday parties aren't just a way for me to show off. They're for my kids. And their friends. And if I feel like showing off that's fine, but my FIRST priority will always be figuring out super fun ways to entertain a bunch of rugrats.

So to answer my friend's question: What's the theme of Holden's birthday party?

Well, the tablecloths are sports because I had leftover ones in our closet, the plates and napkins are LEGO because I had extras from a BBQ last year, the party favors are whatever I pick up at the Dollar Tree that aren't noisy or messy, the decorations are nature because the party's in the backyard, and the cake is whatever cake they have in the fridge at the grocery store that they hopefully have time to write Happy Birthday on because I'll probably forget to order one in advance. But there will be a sprinkler and a Slip 'N Slide and a huge bin of toys and water balloons and squirt guns and chalk and whatever else the kids want to grab from the garage.

I don't know what the other parents will think of my "theme," but whatever. I don't care what they think. I care about what the kids think. They'll have a blast, and that's all that matters. To me at least.

KID'S BIRTHDAY PARTY

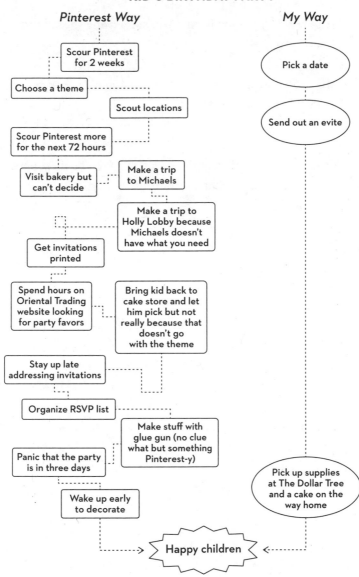

Pinterest Way

- Scour Pinterest for 2 weeks
- Choose a theme
- Scout locations
- Scour Pinterest more for the next 72 hours
- Visit bakery but can't decide
- Make a trip to Michaels
- Make a trip to Holly Lobby because Michaels doesn't have what you need
- Get invitations printed
- Spend hours on Oriental Trading website looking for party favors
- Bring kid back to cake store and let him pick but not really because that doesn't go with the theme
- Stay up late addressing invitations
- Organize RSVP list
- Make stuff with glue gun (no clue what but something Pinterest-y)
- Panic that the party is in three days
- Wake up early to decorate

My Way

- Pick a date
- Send out an evite
- Pick up supplies at The Dollar Tree and a cake on the way home

Happy children

ME: Hey, do you guys want to do something special this
     morning?!
KIDS: Yeahhh!!!
ME: Everyone on your bikes. We're going on a park crawl.
KIDS: What's that?
ME: You'll see.

We all got on our bikes and I led them to the farthest park in
our town, where we played for about fifteen minutes.

ME: Time to go!!
KIDS: Nooooo!
ME: To the next park!!
KIDS: Yayyyyyy!

So we got on our bikes and rode toward our house and
stopped at the next park on the way, and we played there for
about fifteen minutes. And then we rode to another park. And
then another and another. Until we'd hit about five or six parks
on the way home and we were at the last one just down the street
from our house, where we played for about fifteen minutes before riding home. A park crawl! It may not be as wild and crazy as
a pub crawl, but it's equally fun. And instead of feeling like crap
the next day, you feel like the best parent on earth.

This morning Zoey cornered me in the bathroom.

ZOEY: Mom, I need you to tell me the truth.
ME: About what?
ZOEY: About the fairies.

Ruh-rohhhh. I know where she's getting this from. Last night Holden built a fairy house out of LEGOs and left them a note saying *Dear Farees, plees kum* (side note: This would make a horrible title for a porn film). So of course last night the fairies came and visited and left a little of their pixie dust behind.

ZOEY: Mom, was it you? Are you the fairy?

Oh noooo, the magic is gone for her! What should I say? So I looked into her little eyes and this is what I said very loudly.

ME: (loudly) Zoey, Holden put a lot of work into his fairy house and that is why the fairies came to his room and not yours. If you want the fairies to come to your room, you can build something special for them yourself!

But the whole time I was saying that very loudly, I had a mischievous grin on my face and I kept winking at her. I knew Holden was outside the door listening. And then I leaned over and whispered something really quietly in her ear.

ME: Do you want to be my fairy helper from now on?

She quietly did a little celebration dance.

ZOEY: (loud so Holden could hear) Okay, I guess I was just jealous and wish the fairies came to *my* room!!

As soon as Holden was busy downstairs, I let her sprinkle a little "pixie dust" for the first time. And I'm pretty sure she felt like being the fairy helper was equally as exciting as believing in fairies.

- - - - - - - - -

ONE LAST THING:
THAT TIME (OR TIMES)
I TURNED INTO
THE TASMANIAN DEVIL

It happened last week. I don't know WTF came over me, but we had some friends coming over the next day and it was like a switch flipped in my head and suddenly I was possessed by some cleaning demon that needed the entire house to be cleaned right that very moment. I started picking crap up off the counters, throwing shoes in the shoe bins, putting away dishes, scrubbing the pot my hubby left soaking in the sink three days ago, and passive-aggressively throwing everyone's things on the stairs so they could bring them up to their rooms later (which never F'ing works). And at some point in the middle of my rage cleaning, I got even ragier because I could hear them all having fun. Zoey was on an iPhone watching YouTube videos and my hubby was downstairs with Holden watching football and I was like WTF, why am I the only one cleaning? So I started yelling at all of them to immediately stop what they were doing and GET IN HERE RIGHT NOW to help me clean.

> ME: Zoey, you need to clean your guinea pig cage and your room and take a bath and do your homework.
> ZOEY: But I only have 17 seconds left of my video!!
> ME: You can watch it when you're done. Holden, you need to clean up all the scrap paper you left on the table and

cut your nails and I want you to put away all the stuff on the stairs and hang up your laundry.

HOLDEN: But that Peter Pan book isn't mine.

ME: (in my scariest Cujo voice) I DON'T CARE WHOSE IT IS. JUST CLEAN IT UP!!!

And after about twenty minutes of me being insane and them trying to appease me, which was completely impossible, I stopped dead in my tracks. Hold on. WTF is wrong with me? I'm like a combination of Mrs. Hannigan, the Tasmanian Devil, and Cruella de Vil right now. So I took a deep breath, opened Zoey's bedroom door, and saw her quickly stop playing with her LEGOs and pretend to start putting stuff away. The "me" of ten seconds ago would have jumped down her throat, but I was trying to be normal again.

ME: This looks good enough.

And then I walked downstairs and calmly asked Holden if he wanted me to cut his nails while they unpaused the football game and started watching it again. And that stuff on the stairs? I left it and told everyone it just had to be cleaned up before bedtime. And I wondered whether maybe I was insane. Did my mom ever do stuff like this when I was little? I can't remember her having these moments, but she must have, right? Hmmm.

When I think about growing up, I remember other moments. I remember driving in the station wagon and as we approached our house, my mom would tell us to press our noses to open the garage door, and she would secretly press the garage door remote at the same time so we thought our noses were magic. I remember waking up on Sunday mornings and having to search for donuts that were hidden somewhere in the house because the donut fairy had visited the night before. I remember coming into the kitchen and my dad telling us we needed to take our vitamins and handing us each a small handful of "vitamins" (chocolate chips). I don't remember my mom ever having freak-out crazy moments like I did the other day, even though I'm sure she must have once or twice.

And I'm praying my kids are like me. That they forget the moments I freaked out and demanded they clean the house top to bottom, and that they remember the fun moments. Like when Holden and I were having dinner together last week and I turned our regular boring dinner into a date night by setting our places at either end of the long dining room table and putting a few candles in the middle and using the fancy glassware. Or when Zoey came in while I was doing my makeup to go out last week and I said, "Hey, Zoey, can you do my makeup for me?" Or how I bought a girl elf because the kids thought our boy elf needed a friend. And like a million other fun things I did just because I thought they would like it.

As moms, 99 percent of what we do is taking care of our responsibilities. The "have to's" and "need to's" and deadlines and bills and activities and carpools and forms and appointments, etc. etc. etc., and it's easy to forget to have fun. It's easy to become that rage-aholic mom who never stops cleaning or working or grocery-shopping or yelling at the rest of her family to pitch in. And even though it seems insane to add one more thing to my to-do, I'm doing it.

Because I don't want to forget to have fun. And most of all, I want the kids to remember I did.

————o————

Getting Through School Isn't Brain Surgery. It's Harder.

HERE ARE A FEW THINGS that come to mind when I think of school. Math, reading, science, P.E., recess, social studies. And here are a few more things. Bullying, budget cuts, anxiety, social media, vaping, coming out, coming out on a YouTube video that gets millions of views, and lockdowns. Yup, school is like some super complicated shit these days. And if I feel that way as an adult, I can only imagine how overwhelming it must be for kids. I mean, my rugrats are only in elementary school but I can already feel junior high looming like a giant tidal wave, and everything I do between now and when that tidal wave hits is gonna determine whether my rugrats sink or swim. Dear God, I hope I'm giving them the life jacket they're gonna need to survive.

When my kids were little I would complain about something like explosive poopy diapers or pacifier withdrawal to one of my friends who had older kids, and I'd hear the same thing over and over again. "Just you wait. Bigger kids, bigger problems." And I was like A) Screw you for making me feel worse, and B) There's no way it's gonna be harder than this. Well, to anyone who ever told me "bigger kids, bigger problems," I would now like to apologize for cursing you in my head. I was wrong. You were right. Although I'd like to petition that the phrase gets changed to "bigger kids, holy crap this sucks even worse."

So yeah, the older my kiddos get and the more complicated school gets, the more I'm tempted to homeschool them so they don't have to walk into a Roman coliseum every day and battle it out for their lives, but then I'm like WTF are we paying all these taxes for if I don't send them to school and don't you need to have a ton of kids and wear long skirts and bonnets and look like you live on a prairie if you're gonna homeschool? Nahhh, I'm just kidding, but I am 2,000 percent sure I am NOT cut out to be a homeschooling parent. For all sorts of reasons. Like I look at my first grader's math homework and I feel like I need to breathe into a brown paper bag. So for now I send my kids off to school, and while a huge part of me is like woo-hoo, they're in someone else's hands 35 hours a week, the other part of me is like holy crap, I feel like I just sent them into the lion's den. Ruh-roh.

\- - - - - - - - -

FRIEND: When do your kids go back to school?
ME: 17 days, 22 hours, 16 minutes, and 24 seconds. (pause)
17 days, 22 hours, 16 minutes, and 23 seconds. (pause) 17
days, 22 hours, 16 minutes, and 22 seconds. (pause) Not
that I'm counting.

- - - - - - - - -

Dear Teacher,
I hope you don't mind but I don't give teachers an end-of-the-year gift. I give them a beginning-of-the-year gift.

- - - - - - - - -

TEN THINGS TO TELL
YOUR KIDS BEFORE
THEY GO BACK TO SCHOOL

Dear kiddo,

Here it comes, Mommy's favorite day of the year. Back to schoooooool!!!!! And I know we've been shopping all over the place trying to find a three-ringed chartreuse binder and a red panda lunchbox, but really I want to give you something much more important than anything we can buy at a store. Advice. Awww shit, I didn't even know your eyes could roll that far back into your head. I know, I know, the last thing you want to do is listen to your lame mom droning on and on about what you should or shouldn't do, so I'll try to make this quick. Just let your eyes glaze over while I talk but please keep your ears open. Here goes. Ten little pieces of advice that might help you in school and maybe for the rest of your life:

1. Kill everyone with kindness. EVERYONE. Because the people who need it the most are usually the ones you want to give it to the least.
2. Don't have a best friend. Have a few best friends. That way when your best friend is out sick or mad at you, you'll still have a best friend to turn to.

3. Walk down the school hallway like a badass. The very first thing people notice isn't braces or glasses or a zit. It's self-confidence.
4. Don't worry about what you've heard about your teacher ahead of time. There's only one opinion that matters. Yours.
5. Don't save seats at the lunch table. Unless you're saving a seat for someone no one ever saves seats for.
6. Friendship necklaces aren't a way to show that you're best friends with someone. They're a way to make other people feel left out.
7. Make sure to raise your hand in class and speak up — to answer a question if you know it, or ask a question if you don't.
8. Try to help the *new* kids feel like *old* kids.
9. Don't freak out over too much homework. Freaking out doesn't make it go away. It just takes time and energy away from doing it.
10. I love you.

FRIEND: What are you going to do now that both of your kids are in school full time?
ME: Walk around the house saying "Fuck" as much as I want.

MAD LIBS FOR TEACHERS

Dear _____ (parent's name),

    Tonight while I'm sitting on the couch with my _____ (favorite drink), I'll definitely be thinking about your kid _____ (child's name).

I am so _____ (adjective) you gave birth to that little _____ (noun). _____ (He/She) makes my life as a teacher extra _____ (adjective). Like that time _____ (child's name) came to school and _____ (past tense verb) in the classroom and made all the other students _____ (verb). Those are the moments that make me want to _____ (verb). So when you're thinking about my gift for _____ (upcoming holiday), feel free to buy me lots of _____ (favorite drink or drug) or just a gift card to _____ (favorite store) for _____ (amount of money).

When _____ (child's name) graduates, you better bet I'll be _____ (verb that ends with –ing).

                     Sincerely,

        _____ (teacher's name)

- - - - - - - - -

THE TIME ZOEY GOT A HAIRCUT
SHE DIDN'T ASK FOR

Zoey came home from school the other day and was walking through the kitchen when I noticed something.

ME: Zoey, what happened to your hair?
ZOEY: What?
ME: Did you cut it?
ZOEY: (panic) WHAT?!!!

Based on her reaction I immediately realized she had no idea what I was talking about. So I knew she probably didn't cut it herself (unlike the last time). I could see she was starting to freak out.

ZOEY: What's wrong with my hair?!
ME: Ummm, it just looks like a little chunk of your hair was, uhhh, cut in the back.

I didn't want to make a big deal out of it because I didn't want to upset her, and to be honest I was trying to hide that I was freaking out a little. I mean, it was a pretty good chunk. Probably about 50 or more hairs were cut in a straight line about an inch from her scalp right around where a high ponytail would be. And it was sticking up like Alfalfa. I would show you what it looks like but there's no way in hell I was going to make her upset by taking a picture of it.

ZOEY: I don't want to have short hair!! I like my hair!!!
ME: It's not short, honey. It's just one tiny little place. I promise. Can you think of how your hair might have gotten cut?
ZOEY: No.
ME: Were you guys using scissors at school today?
ZOEY: Yes. But who cut it? Who would do something so mean?
ME: I don't know, honey.

For the rest of the afternoon, Zoey had this sad look on her face. And I was sad for her. Luckily I was able to part her hair on the other side and brush it over the section to hide it, but that didn't turn her frown upside down. Because her sadness was less about her hair and more about feeling violated by one of her friends. There are only 18 kids in her class and she really thinks of each one of them as a friend. No enemies. No girl drama. Eighteen friends.

Of course I immediately reached out to her teacher and we talked about it a lot. She had no idea who would have done that, and she even drove back to school that evening to look for any clues before the custodian cleaned. Nothing.

The next morning Zoey was still thinking about it.

ZOEY: Mom, did they find out who did it?

I can't blame her. I'd want to know the same thing.

ME: No, honey. We might not ever know.
ZOEY: I just want to know *why* they did it.
ME: I know WHY they did it.
ZOEY: You do?! Why???
ME: Because they're hurting in here (I pat my chest). Zoey, I want you to listen to me carefully right now. I know you feel embarrassed, but this is not about YOU. This is about them. This is about someone else feeling so bad on the inside that they did something bad to you.

And she sat there for a moment thinking about it.

ZOEY: I feel sorry for them.

Yup, that's when I knew she got it. She GOT it. People who do bad things usually do it because they feel bad on the inside.

And I think it made her feel better. I mean, she didn't start smiling on the spot or anything, but she finished getting ready for school, brushed her hair like nothing was wrong, and was laughing by the time she headed out the door. And she never mentioned it again.

She'll probably never learn who cut her hair, but I kinda think she learned something more important: That even if you're nice to everyone, someone might still be so angry that they take their pain out on you. And that sucks. Whether it's a kid with a scissors or a kid with something else. All we can do is keep being nice, keep smiling, keep trying to help other people, and keep hoping it's enough.

Take a bully away, and you fix your kiddo's problem. Teach your kiddo to handle a bully, and you fix it for a lifetime.

HOW I WISH MY CONVERSATION WITH THE SCHOOL NURSE WOULD GO WHEN I KNOW MY KID IS FAKING IT

(ring ring)

ME: Hello?

NURSE: Everything is okay. This is the school nurse. Zoey got kicked in the arm in P.E. but she's fine.

ME: Like totally fine?

NURSE: Totally fine. She has a bad case of fake-arm-ititis. She's being extra dramatic and wants to come home but I told her to shake it off because I know that's what you would do.

ME: Thanks. You can also tell her if she comes home she won't be getting any screen time and she'll just have to entertain herself all day and I'll be passive-aggressively grumpy.

NURSE: I will. And how about I tell her if she comes home, she'll be paying you back for this day of school?

ME: It's public school. It doesn't cost anything.

NURSE: But she doesn't know that.

ME: Brilliant. Go for it.

NURSE: Great.

ME: I'll see you later when I drop off a bottle of wine for you.

NURSE: Awww, you don't have to do that.

ME: Yes, I do. For handling my kid the same way I would.

- - - - - - - - -

YOUR HEAD WILL
ITCH AFTER READING
THIS CHAPTER

My head is itching. My head is itching!!!! WHY IS MY HEAD ITCHING?!!!! Oh yeahhhh, I know, because I just got the lice letter. The dreaded F'ing lice letter.

What it says:

Dear parent,
    A lice infestation has been detected in a student in your child's classroom. Please read the attached information sheet about pediculus humanus capitis and how to handle it.

What it should say:

You're fucked.

Have you ever seen what a lice (louse???) looks like. If not, go Google it right now. Crap, wait, never mind, do NOT Google it because it will haunt your nightmares for the rest of your life. Awwww shit, is it too late, did you already Google it before I told you not to? Sorry not sorry, because now at least you know what to look for. Which is kinda hilarious since I'm sorry, but if you saw one of these things crawling on your kid's head and didn't know what it was, you would still freak the F out and would not just brush that motherF'er off. You'd shave your kid's head and then burn it. Not the louse. Your kid's head. Sorry, honey, you're gonna have to go to school without a head tomorrow.

Side note: I'd like to apologize for cursing so much in this chapter but if you've ever gotten lice in your household, you know that you do not use words like "awwww dookie" when you're talking about lice. You'd say words like "MotherF'ingSon-ofaBitchwithatwistofOhhFuckThisShit." And yes, that's a real word. You know when Merriam put it in her dictionary? Right after she burned her house to the ground because her kid got lice.

So the school sends home the lice letter and here's what goes through your very itchy head. WHO is the kid who has it? Not that you really care who it is because of course you're not going to ostracize them or anything (oh hells yeah you are), but because you need to know some super important shit. Like does my kid play with Little Miss Liceypants? Are their desks next to each other? Has she been to my house lately? Has she slept over in the past two years? Was she the kid who was head-butting my kid in the carpool line last week?

Oh, and the oh-so-handy info sheet the school sends you is gonna say something like, "Carefully comb through your child's hair to detect if there are any nits."

Bwahahahahaha, nits. Nits my ass. The word "nits" is just a happy bullshit word for what they really are. Eggs. People, nits are motherF'ing BUG EGGS. As in eggs that squirted out of a bug's vajayjay. And in order to find the bug eggs in your kid's hair, you have to have like super bionic x-ray vision. Because they basically look like itty-bitty minuscule pieces of dandruff clinging to their hair near the scalp that you will never notice. But that's okay because if you don't see the eggs, it'll be super easy to find them in a week or so when THEY HATCH!!!! BARFFFFF!!!! And then you'll definitely notice real live bugs weaving in and out of your kid's hair shafts like the orange cones in P.E. class. And you know what they're doing in there? Laying more eggs. Yup, it's a vicious cycle.

And speaking of cycles, wanna know what else is a cycle? Once you've washed every sheet, blanket, towel, and pillowcase in your house on high heat and done 9,000 loads of laundry and bagged every stuffed animal that lives in your life-sized claw machine, guess what happens? A month later it's basically that scene in *The Shining*. Picture a little louse axing through the bathroom door and poking his head into the room where you're hiding. I'm baaccccccckkkkkkk. MotherF'ingSonofaBitchwithatwist-ofOhhFuckThisShitAgain. Yup, just because you get all the lice out of your house the first time doesn't mean you can't get it again. And again. And again. Because lice is not like the chicken pox. And because Little Miss Liceypants's mom didn't vacuum her sofa and Little Miss Liceypants got lice again and brought it back into the classroom and headbutted your kid at recess and her louse went leapfrogging from head to head to head. Awesome.

So even though you literally just took Stuffy Puffy the Penguin out of the trash bag and gave him back to your kiddo, now you have to wrench him out of your love muffin's vise grip again and shove him back into a trash bag for two more weeks. And rewash every sheet, towel, blanket, and pillowcase. And vacuum the sofa. And march down the street to Little Miss Liceypants's house and do alllll their shit too so you can end the vicious lice cycle.

The moral of this story: homeschool your kids. Seriously, I used to wonder why people homeschooled until lice happened in our house. And now I know. If you homeschool your douchenuggets, you might have to deal with them 24 hours a day and teach them math and science and reading and Spanish, but you will never ever get the dreaded lice letter. Now excuse me while I go get some Band-Aids because my head is bleeding because I can't stop scratching it.

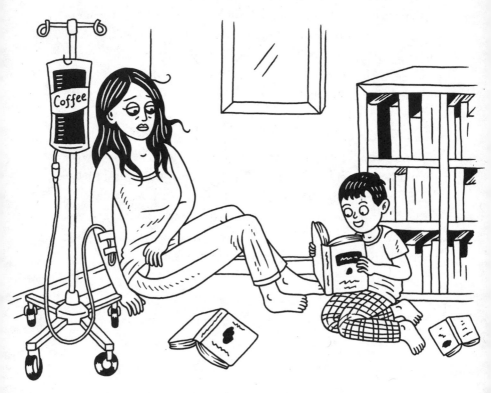

One day I'm going to invent a podcast to help insomniacs fall asleep and it's just going to be recordings of kindergartners and first-graders learning how to read.

WOULD YOU RATHER FIND OUT:

A. Your kid stuffed someone in a locker

B. Your kid got stuffed in a locker

C. No one got stuffed in a locker because your kid stopped
it from happening

CORRECT ANSWER: C, BUT SOMETIMES I WORRY
ABOUT D. YOUR KID GOT STUFFED IN A LOCKER
TOO BECAUSE THEY TRIED TO STOP IT FROM
HAPPENING.

I'M SORRY I CALLED YOUR KID A DICKHEAD BUT IN ALL FAIRNESS, HE WAS BEING A DICKHEAD

Dear mom who will remain unnamed,

WTF? I can't believe what I just heard. That your
dickhead kid was purposely switching stuff in people's
lockers. I mean, seriously? I blamed Holden for losing
his hoodie again and kept telling him he was going to
have to pay me back for the hoodie, but then yesterday
he finally came home with it and I was like where did
you find it and you know what he said? That apparently
the school busted YOUR kid for taking people's crap
out of lockers and purposely putting it in other people's.
And honestly, I'm not surprised.

I mean, it was YOUR kid who purposely kicked the ball on the roof at recess. It was YOUR kid who kept flicking my kid's head while they were in line in the hallway. It's YOUR kid whose name I hear day after day after day because he's constantly disrupting class and making the teacher lose her shit and making it harder for my kid to learn. My kid can't read yet, and I'm blaming it on your kid. No, wait, I'm blaming it on you. For letting your kid be such a little douchenugget.

And just when I thought I was going to blow a gasket if I heard one more thing about YOUR kid, I heard one more thing.

So this morning I'm telling my friend about your kid's locker switcheroo game and guess what she tells me? She tells me you're sick of it too. That you've been taking him to a therapist, and seeing a therapist yourself, and just started him on some medicine and are basically trying every single thing you can possibly do to turn your little dickhead into a kid who's *not* the kid everyone curses at the dinner table every night. She tells me that you're trying. Hard.

And suddenly something in my head changes. Like a light switch. Suddenly he's not a little dickhead anymore. Now he's just a kid who has some issues that need a little extra TLC and patience. And you're not a shitty parent anymore either. Now you're a parent who's trying your hardest to rein in a kid who's a little out of control in a world that's probably judging him a lot and yelling at him a lot and constantly giving him negative reinforcement.

So I'm sorry. I'm sorry for calling him a little dickhead. The things he's doing might be dickheady, but that doesn't make him a dickhead. And maybe it's not your parenting style that's F'ing him up at all. Maybe your parenting style is flipping awesome and maybe without it he would eventually turn into a loser a-hole who never fits in. But because you're working so hard and putting in the effort now, you're gonna nip this thing in the bud and raise an amazing kid who will eventually turn into an amazing adult. I mean, who knows?! Maybe he'll become the scientist who cures cancer, or the president of the United States, or the winner of the Nobel Peace Prize. Or at least just not the kid that everyone curses at the dinner table every night.

> Signing off with lots of love and
> support and a new perspective,
> A mom who knows you're trying
> and that speaks volumes

Recently Zoey's started doing this really annoying thing. Whenever I'm reading Harry Potter to her, she corrects me if I miss a word or say an extra one. But tonight I decided I shouldn't be annoyed by this at all. Because it means she's reading along. Which means she's perfectly capable of reading Harry Potter herself now that she's older, but still chooses to read it WITH me.

IF YOUR KID FORGETS THEIR LUNCHBOX, DO YOU:

A. Stop whatever you're doing and rush it over to the school

B. Get McDonald's delivered to them and stink up the entire school with mouthwatering french-fry smell

C. Text the teacher and beg her to share a little of her lunch with them

D. Let your kiddo fend for themselves and teach them not to forget their lunch next time

CORRECT ANSWER: I WANT TO SAY D BECAUSE I KNOW THAT'S THE RIGHT ANSWER, BUT I'M MORE LIKELY TO DO A.

ZOEY: Mom, what if people make fun of me for having an expander?

ME: Zoey, like half your grade has one.

ZOEY: Not half.

ME: Fine, a lot of people.

ZOEY: But what if they make fun of ME today?

ME: You just say to them, "You're just jealous."

ZOEY: Mommm, NO ONE wants an expander. They wouldn't be jealous of it.

ME: No, I mean, "You're just jealous of how awesome I'm going to look."

ZOEY: Ohhh, good one.

ME: And then spin around and walk away like you own the school.

ZOEY: Like this?

ME: Just like that.

Bullies gonna bully. But badasses are gonna badass.

ONE LAST THING:
THE THING THAT WORKS WAYYYY
BETTER THAN LOCKDOWN DRILLS

ME: Hey, buddy, how was school today?
HOLDEN: Fine.

Shit shit shit, you NEVER ask "How was school?" You ask questions like "What did you do in P.E.?" or "What are you making in art class?" *Specific* questions.

ME: Just fine? Okay, let's try it this way. How was math? Did you get your spelling quiz back? Did you have music? Was recess outside? Name every single person you sat by at the lunch table. Did you play with that Carl kid? Why don't you play with that Duncan kid tomorrow? Were you cold without a jacket? Did you get in trouble at all?

You bombard them with specific questions. And sometimes they give you an answer like this.

HOLDEN: I don't remember.

And sometimes they have verbal diarrhea.

HOLDEN: We got to play steal the jewels in P.E. and I
stole them a bunch and . . .

He's so excited he can't stop talking. But then there are other
days.

HOLDEN: We had a lockdown drill and we had to hide
behind the desks and have our water bottles ready to
throw just in case.

And your heart skips a beat. Like it literally clenches up because WTF is a kid going to do with a water bottle if someone
gets into their school with a gun? It's heartbreaking. It's basically terrorism for little kids. But here's the thing: the fear is so
much greater than the numbers. That's not to say the problem
shouldn't be addressed, but honestly:
More kids die from suicide every year.
More kids die in auto accidents every year.
More kids die from suffocation, drowning, poison, fires, cancer, and falling every year. Awwww shit, I was trying to help you
feel better about lockdown drills but now you're just worrying
about the tons of ways your kid can die. Sorry, my bad. Send me
your Prozac bill for today.
All I'm saying is that it sucks that our kids have to do these
drills at school, but instead of worrying about them and putting
our energy into freaking out every time we turn on the news and
see a line of kids marching out of their school with their hands
on their heads (gulp), we're much better off putting our energy

into our own kids. Checking in on them, staying close to them, keeping an eye on what they're doing on their screens and cell phones and behind closed doors, letting them know they can *always* talk to you, protecting them physically (by locking up our guns if we have them) and emotionally (by asking *specific* questions about how their day *really* was). And hopefully if we each do our job, there will be way fewer reasons to have lockdown drills in the first place.

——o——

Whatta You Mean Your Kid's Not Training for the Olympics?

OKAY, SO HERE'S THE DEALIO. If you want your rugrat to be good at something, you have to sign them up to do it by the time they're three years old. And since you don't know what they're gonna like or be good at, you have to sign them up for pretty much every single activity that exists just to try them all out. And you're gonna have to shell out a boatload of cash to pay for it all. And you're gonna have to act like a total crazy person on the sidelines and yell at the coach and referee a lot, and maybe even throw some punches at other parents sometimes. And you're gonna have to travel like every single weekend and you might even have to pull them out of school for tournaments and stuff. But hey, what's more important? School or giving your kid the best chance to become captain of the cheerleaders or a violin virtuoso or an Olympic athlete?

Ummmm, I'm gonna go with school. Because unless your kid is the next Lebron James, the purpose of after-school activities isn't to turn your kids into professional athletes or halftime dancers. It's to help them develop self-esteem, teach them how to be team players, and keep them *so* busy they don't have time to get high on Cartoon Network or ~~marijuanah~~ ~~marajuana~~, how the hell do you spell that word? Fine, pot.

So are after-school activities important? Yup. Yup. Yup. They exercise kids' muscles and brains and passions and creative spirits. But there are people who are gonna act like if your kid doesn't figure out her "thing" by the time she's chewing on her mortarboard tassel at the preschool graduation, then she's F'ed. She's gonna be shut out. Don't believe the hype.

There are parents who are gonna show up to every basketball game with their kiddo's name painted across their chest (slight exaggeration, VERY slight). There are parents who are going to "casually mention" in every single conversation that their kid has been playing the violin since they were in the womb (ohhh, did you literally shove a violin up your hoo-ha to get Baby Placenta started early?). There are parents who are going to "complain" about alllllll the driving they have to do from one sport to another, and the reason the word "complain" is in quotation marks is that they aren't really complaining. They're bragging. These parents are very loud and it will be very hard to ignore them, but try to.

Because look around. Are most of your grownup friends professional soccer players? Or prima ballerinas? Or professional chess players? Nope. They're accountants and lawyers and store managers and nurses and police officers, etc. etc. etc., and they have regular, fulfilling, decent-paying jobs. And maybe they play in an adult league or something, but the activities they did as kids really aren't their life. They're just a part of their life. The same way it should be when they're kids.

- - - - - - - - - -

Did you know that Tom Brady won every single game he played in the second grade?!*

*Completely made up because no one remembers or gives a shit because he was 8 and elementary school games do not matter so calm the F down.

- - - - - - - - -

YO, MR. BUTTHEAD,
THIS IS WHY KIDS PLAY SPORTS

So the other day I'm standing on the sidelines at a soccer game and I can't help but notice this father who keeps yelling things at his kid like "Stop being such a sissy!" and "Get in there and score a goal already!!" and "I only buy ice cream for winners!" Oh noooo you didn't. Did he seriously just say ice cream is only for winners? Helllloooo, the most important time to buy your kid ice cream is when they're feeling bad because they lost (or when Mommy really wants some).

Anyways, I wanted to shake this dad and yell, "Aggghhh, take a chill pill!! You're missing the point!!!" Contrary to what you think, Mr. Butthead, the goal of elementary school soccer is *not* that big net your kid is trying to kick the ball into. I mean, yeah, technically that's a goal, but winning is only one eensy-weensy, itty-bitty part of why kids play sports. Because even if they walk away from the field (or court, or stage, or rink, or ring, or pool, or beam, etc. etc. etc.) without a win, they're walking away with a crapload of other awesome things:

1. Fun. I know it sounds cliché, but seriously (or rather unseriously), your kid is kicking an inflated ball around on a big plot of grass. If they're not having fun, what's the F'ing point?

2. Good sportsmanship. You know when the kids line up at the end of the game to slap hands and say "good game"? They're learning to put their differences aside after a big fight. I know grownups who can't even do that.

3. How to lose. Not how to be a LOSER. How to be a WINNER when you lose. You can sulk a little, you can be bummed, but after about five or ten minutes, it's time to pick yourself up and keep going. To the ice cream shop.

4. How to win. There's a right way to win: "Woo-hoo, we won!!! Good game!!!" And there's a wrong way to win: "In your face!! Nah nah nah nah, hey hey hey, goodbye!!" The same way losers can be winners, winners can be losers. The problem is, winners who are losers keep being losers their whole lives even when they're not playing sports anymore.

5. Exercise!! Wanna know something amazing?! The kids that run around the field and score two goals burn the same number of calories as the kids that run around the field and score six goals. So even though winning might be good for your ego, winning AND losing are good for your heart, lungs, muscles, tendons, and midsection.

6. How to be a team player. If that person hadn't kicked the goal, they wouldn't have won. But if that other person hadn't passed him the ball in the first place, they wouldn't have won either.

7. Respect. If they don't listen to the coach, they don't play. If they don't listen to the ref, they don't play. And one day many years from now, whether their boss is the head of the NFL, a Fortune company, or the local supermarket, if they don't listen to their boss, they don't play.

8. Something to do other than drugs and video games. When you're busy playing sports, you're too busy to do other stuff—shit that'll make you high or a couch potato. I mean, sure, you'll have awesome reflexes . . . to quickly call 911 when you have a heart attack at age 42.

9. How to shake it off. I mean, sure, you could just learn it from the Taylor Swift song, but it's really not the same thing as getting a swift kick to the cojones and staying in the game.

10. Cheering from the bench, eating a good breakfast, not bugging the coach to put you in, remembering all of your equipment, how to keep going even when you're being pummeled, practice practice practice, playing until you hear the whistle, and last but not least, the importance of putting your dirty uniform in the washer if you have a game the next day.

DEAR WOMAN SITTING NEXT TO ME AT THE ICE RINK

Dear woman sitting next to me at the ice rink,

Wow, I can't believe you just did that. I mean, I've sat on the sidelines next to sooo many parents, but I've never seen someone do that before. And I thought I'd seen it all. Parents who bitch out the ref, parents who heckle little kids, parents who get in blowout fights with other parents, parents who push other people down to get a good seat, parents who act like kindergarten basketball is the NBA, etc. etc. etc.

But when I went to Zoey's ice skating competition and randomly sat down next to you, I was totally caught off guard. The way you leaned over and whispered to me, "Do you want me to take a video of your daughter when she skates her routine so you can just watch her skate?" You want to what?! I meannnn, our kids are competing against each other. You're not supposed to be nice to me. You're supposed to give me the bitchy side-eye until I catch you so you flash me a fake smile and ask what song my daughter's skating to even though you really couldn't give a rat's tushie. But nope, you were nice. Like genuinely nice. And I can't tell you how much it means to me.

I spend every race, every game, every competition recording my kids to show to our relatives, which means that even though I'm at the events, I'm constantly watching my kids through a screen. Trying to line them up in the frame, moving the phone to follow them, cursing every time I miss a goal or a waltz jump or a line in a play, or kicking myself for forgetting to push record. But not today. Because of you, today I have the most awesome video of my daughter skating *and* I also have the most awesome memory of watching my daughter skate. Live. Not through a screen.

So I want to say thanks. There should be more parents on the sidelines like you. There to support our kids AND each other.

Sincerely,
A mom who will pay it forward to another
mom at the next competition

OMG, Holden had his first soccer game and this other player kicked his ass. This kid was a powerhouse, and ridiculously fast, and just kept pummeling the ball and making goals over and over again. Talk about a badass. Oh, and BTW, she was a girl. I love that kindergarten soccer is still coed. It teaches my son that girls are a force to be reckoned with.

TIP: When I sign my kids up for an activity and they end up not liking it, I usually let them quit because A) I've already spent the money so it's gone anyway, and B) I don't see it as teaching them to quit. I see it as teaching them to walk away from something that doesn't make them happy (cough cough, future bad boyfriends and crappy jobs).

- - - - - - - - -

WHAT NOT TO DO
WHEN YOU ARE AT YOUR
KID'S HOLIDAY CONCERT

Okay, so here's a question. Which would you rather do? Lick the cake batter bowl and get salmonella and have diarrhea for 48 hours straight OR go to your kid's beginners' orchestra concert? Be tortured in one orifice or another? I would pick diarrhea. I shit you not. Well, I guess I do shit you . . . for 48 hours. Don't get me wrong, I know that it's amazing, wonderful, fantastic, spectacular when a kid wants to play an instrument and it helps shape their brain in all kinds of amazing ways. I just truly believe it should be done on a remote island in the South Pacific for the first seven years they're learning the instrument before anyone else should be subjected to it.

But alas, not only did I have to listen to Zoey practice her viola at home (only if I made her, which I did not), I also had to go to her first beginners' orchestra concert and sit for an hour and pretend like it was amazing. But hey, by this point in my kid's life,

I was used to being tortured and I was basically a professional expert at getting through shit like this.

Little did I know the worst part about attending one of these things has nothing to do with listening to a bunch of kids playing instruments. Nope. The torture actually starts long before the kids even take the stage.

Because when you get to the concert (no matter how early you arrive), the first thing you'll notice is that the first 20 rows have been saved by some asshat who's invited every living relative they have and for some reason they think their great-aunt-in-law Ida should get a seat that's better than yours.

Oh, and there are one of two ways this asshat will save said shitload of seats:

A. With actual tape because they literally brought a roll along specifically to save entire rows of seats

Or B. With any little thing they can find in their pockets because they forgot their roll of tape

YOU: Is this seat taken?

THEM: Duhh, don't you see I put a breath mint on it?

But just you wait because the fun hasn't even started yet. Here come the kids! And not only does your view suck because Aunt Ida's pink bouffant is blocking it, but now you're dealing with something else too. Nine thousand people holding up their giant screens to record their rugrats. And the only way for you to see the concert is to watch it on Uncle Carl's iPad two rows in front of you. And I know what you're thinking. It's a concert, so at least you can still hear the lovely music. FYI, this is not music. It is a beginners' orchestra concert. I just want to SEE (not hear) my child play.

Speaking of hearing things, want to know what sucks? When it's finally your kid's turn and all the people sitting around you are chitchatting because it's not their kid's turn right now. Hellllooooo, when any kid on the stage is playing or singing or dancing or mining for gold in their nose, STFU. Because if you talk you're making it hard for someone to enjoy their kid's performance, *and* your talking will end up in everyone else's videos including mine so the next time I come to one of these things, I *will* think ahead and bring a roll of tape but not to save seats . . . so I can tape your big fat mouth closed.

Anyways, I could keep going on and on and on about the ass-hats who talk, who stand in the aisle to take pictures, who leave as soon as *their own* kid is done, who let the siblings act like jerk-wads in the audience, etc. etc. etc. Because yes, it's true, there are so many things I'd rather be doing than sitting at a beginners' orchestra concert. But I came. And I'm here to be tortured by my kid, not by you.

FRIEND: Hey, want to schedule a playdate?
ME: Definitely! Holden's been dying to have one
    with Lucas.
FRIEND: Tuesday?
ME: Nope, soccer on Tuesday. Wednesday after 5:00?
FRIEND: He has theater at 5:00. Friday?
ME: Basketball game. Monday?
FRIEND: He has a piano lesson and then tennis.
ME: We can't do Thursday.
FRIEND: Neither can we.
ME: How about March 16, 2047?
FRIEND: That works!

WATCHING YOUR KIDDO FAIL IS HEARTBREAKING, EXCRUCIATING, UNBEARABLE, AND TOTALLY AWESOME

OMG, I can't wait to see Zoey, ooooh, I hope she does great!! I'm sitting in the ice rink on a freezing-cold bench (my favorite hemorrhoid will be arriving later today) at the first of four ice skating recitals (apparently one isn't enough torture), there are like 9,000 acts before Zoey's (at least that's what it feels like), but it's finally her turn (insert angels singing here). Holy crap, did I seriously just have four parentheticals in one sentence (my bad)?!

Her group's music starts playing and it's like the curtains are projectile-vomiting little girls in sequined outfits. Where is she?! Which one is Zoey? I'm looking and looking. Finding your kid in an ice-skating recital is like opening a *Where's Waldo?* book but every person on every page is wearing blue pants and a red-and-white striped shirt. All 25 girls are wearing the same exact costume and have their hair in the same high ponytail and they're swarming all over the ice like little bumblebees. Seriously, last week I watched someone else's kid spinning for like 30 minutes before I realized it wasn't mine.

And then I see her. Awwwww, the smile on her face is beaming. And she looks soooo beautiful out there. I mean, don't get me wrong, I know she's not going to the Olympics or anything. Side note: There are two kinds of moms at the ice rink — the ones who realize their kids aren't going to the Olympics and the ones who are like totally cutthroat and truly believe their daughters might suddenly excel at warp speed and launch themselves into the Olympics. Helllllooo people, don't you know, if your kid is good enough to go to the Olympics, a man in a trench coat with a clipboard approaches you when your kid is like three years old and tells you she needs to move far away to train with some fancy coach with a Russian accent (no F'ing idea if this is true, but it's what I imagine happens). But I digress. Back to my subjectively speaking best ice skater ever.

Wow, look at her bunny hop, and look at her crossovers, and look at her jumpy-thingie (I never took ice skating so I don't know WTF to call stuff). And then suddenly she's flying through the air, but NOT in a good way. In the kind of way that her legs are flailing out behind her and she's about three feet off the ice and she's coming down hard.

BAM!

AUDIENCE: Gasp!

She does a total belly flop on the hard ice, and all I can think is, "Oh crap, there goes the nine million dollars we've spent on orthodontia." My heart is in my throat and the girls are skating past her at lightning speed and I'm totally envisioning all their blades slicing off her fingers now. Not my baby!! NOT MY BABY!!! Watching this is brutal.

But wait, what's she doing? She's getting up!! She quickly gets to her feet and goes straight into a beautiful spiral. THAT'S MY DAUGHTER!!!!!! And then she does the best spin I have ever seen her do, and I am bursting with pride that she was able to rebound after her crash. But then . . . awww crap, here we go again.

Yup, she's up in the air and comes down hard, like even harder than before. And she hits the ice with so much force, I can feel it. Oh wait, no, I think what I'm actually feeling is my heart breaking in two for her. I want to leap out of my seat and run to her, but all I can do is sit there watching it unfold while biting off all my fingernails and praying she's okay. Again she gets up just like she's supposed to, and she has to keep on skating for another ten seconds until she strikes the final pose, her arms held victoriously in the air and a huge smile across her face. But it's all fake. I can see the truth in her eyes. They're welling up with tears and she is in pain. It kills me.

As soon as the lights go down, I bolt out of my seat and run to where she exits the rink and this time it's not hard to spot her because there's only one girl who's bawling her eyes out. Mine.

I tell her to take deep breaths, I hug her and tell her I'm so proud of her for finishing the routine, I try to shield her from all the people who keep coming over to ask if she's okay, I hold ice packs on her knees, but she's a wreck and can't stop sobbing and sucking in air. This is a disaster.

I know what she's gonna say. That she's embarrassed and hurt and scared and never wants to go out there again. That she wants to skip the finale and just go home. I mean, I can't really blame her. I'd probably do the same thing.

ZOEY: People are lining up for the finale! Gotta go!

Wait, what? Seriously?! And she tosses her ice packs onto the bench and runs off in her skates while I resist the urge to yell after her to stop running or she might fall. But so what if she does? I know something now. She'll just get back up.

She goes back out on the ice for the finale and doesn't fall once and puts her arms in the air and a smile on her face like she's just won the Olympic gold medal and I am beaming. BEAM-ING. Maybe even more than I would be if she just went out there and never fell in the first place.

After the show we get into the car and I tell her like a thousand times how proud I am of her. I can't stop saying Hallmark-y things like, "Zoey, life tested you today and you passed with a million flying colors." I'm sure she's rolling her eyes in the back seat, but who cares? By the time we get home, she seems recovered. But *I'm* not. I've never had that feeling before. Seeing her get hurt and seeing her emotions get smashed like that was almost unbearable.

And that night as I'm putting her to bed and I'm closing the door to her room, she stops me. "Mom?" Usually I would be annoyed at the stalling tactic, but seeing her tragedy earlier has turned me into the nicest, sweetest, most sympathetic mommy on earth.

ME: What is it, honey?
ZOEY: Do you know what was going through my head
    when I fell?
ME: No, what?
ZOEY: The first time I fell, I thought *oh damn it*, the
    second time I thought *oh shit*, and the third time I
    thought *oh fuck*.
ME: Zoey!!
ZOEY: No, Mom, don't worry. Just inside my head.

Bwahahahaha. This makes me laugh pretty hard and as I'm shutting the door I'm still giggling. She can laugh about it, so I guess I should too.

I never want to have this feeling ever again, but I will. Many, *many* times. Whether she falls on the ice, or because someone dumps her, or because she fails a test, or doesn't get in to the college she wants or the job she applies for, or a million other reasons. I'll have to let her fall, both literally and figuratively. And deep down I know that letting her fall is a good thing, because falling down is the only way she'll learn how to get back up. And if my heart breaks in the meantime, there's always Super Glue. And wine.

- - - - - - - - -

7 AWESOME THINGS YOUR KIDS
LEARN WHEN THEY LOSE

1. How to fight harder the next time.
2. What it's like to be challenged and not have everything just handed to you on a silver platter.
3. How to shake it off *and* shake the other team's hand no matter how much you can't stand them.
4. How to feel good about the way you played and know your performance isn't measured by the score.
5. How to know when the reason you lost is because you didn't play as well as you could have.
6. How your parents aren't disappointed *in* you. They're disappointed *for* you.
7. How it's hard to keep frowning when your mouth is full of ice cream.

You can invest $40,000 in lessons, private coaches, equipment, and tournaments so your kid can *maybe* get a partial scholarship to college.

Or you can invest $40,000 in a 529 plan so they can *definitely* have every penny they need to pay for college and maybe even grad school.

Only one of them is a sure bet. But after you fund the 529 plan, feel free to use the rest for sports. And maybe one of those cushiony butt thingies so you can sit comfortably on the cold hard bleachers.

HOW TO FIND OUT IF
YOU ARE ONE OF THOSE
A-HOLE F-WAD D-BAG
PARENTS ON THE SIDELINES

I know what you're thinking. *"I'm* not one of them." I'm not surprised because A) you're reading my book so you probably ARE totally awesome, but B) people usually aren't willing to admit that they're A-hole F-wad D-bags so you might not even know you are. So before you pull your little foldy chair up next to mine so we can watch the game together and then laugh our asses off at the end of the game when we try to get our asses out of our foldy chairs but have lots of trouble standing up, open your junk drawer and grab a #2 (a pencil, not a piece of poop, unless you find a piece of poop in there, in which case grab it and throw it away) and get ready because we're about to find out if you're a total badass or a total asswipe on the sidelines. Here goes:

I. WHEN THE REFEREE MAKES A CALL THAT YOU DON'T AGREE WITH, DO YOU:

A. Say, oh well, because it's elementary school sports so who gives a shit

B. Say, oh well, because the ref's 19 and hot and whatever he says is sexy

C. Curse loudly until young children around you start crying and the team chips in at the end of the season to buy you a gift certificate to anger management classes

2. WHEN YOUR KID SUCKS AT A SPORT, DO YOU:

A. Cheer for him like he's the best player out there

B. Decide that if he's smiling then he's clearly getting something out of it

C. Shake your head in shame and tell him to quit being such a sissy-loser and never sign him up for *that* sport again

3. WHEN ALL THE OTHER PARENTS ARE SITTING IN CHAIRS TRYING TO WATCH THE GAME, DO YOU:

A. Sit in a chair too

B. Stand behind the chairs because you're too excited to sit down and watch

C. Stand on the sideline right in front of all the other parents and even step on the field sometimes and never once think about the fact that you make a better door than a window, shithead

4. IF YOUR SON IS PLAYING AGAINST A GIRL, DO YOU:
A. Not even really think about it
B. Secretly hope the girl wins to teach your son that girls are F'ing awesome
C. Automatically assume your boy's gonna win, and if he doesn't, yell stuff like, "Seriously? You're gonna let a girl beat you?!"

5. IF YOUR KID HATES SOMETHING SHE SIGNED UP FOR, DO YOU:
A. Encourage her to stick out the season but say she doesn't have to sign up again
B. Let her quit because you've already lost your money, so oh well
C. Drag her ass to every practice and game and force her to play the entire season even though she's sobbing and really had no idea what she was signing up for in the first place because she's too young to know

6. IF YOU FEEL LIKE HAVING A DRINK AT A CHILDREN'S SPORTING EVENT, DO YOU:
A. Bring it in something stealthy and quietly sip it so it's not glaringly obvious
B. Bring enough for all the other parents too, along with a stack of solid cups so you don't all look like lushes
C. Get rip-roaring drunk and act like you're on spring break in college and then jump into your car and peel out of the parking lot at the end of the game with a minivan full of kiddos

7. IF YOU'RE CHATTING WITH THE OTHER PARENTS
ON THE SIDELINES, DO YOU:

A. Try to remember to watch your kid once in a while
   because that's why you're there

B. Feel bad when you miss an awesome play because you
   weren't paying attention and try harder next time

C. Think it's social hour for you and spend all your time
   mingling with the other parents and barely even know
   how the game is going and maybe not even what sport
   you're watching

8. IF YOU DON'T AGREE WITH WHAT THE COACH
IS DOING, DO YOU:

A. Keep your mouth shut because you could have been a
   coach but decided not to

B. Wait until after the game and speak with her privately
   to politely mention your subjective opinion that you
   acknowledge is less important than hers

C. Shout all of your criticisms to her across the field
   like a total jerkwad and ignore that she's either
   volunteering or probably being paid very little to take
   care of your kid

9. IF YOUR TEAM IS KICKING THE OTHER TEAM'S ASS AND THE SCORE IS LIKE A MILLION TO ZERO, DO YOU:

A. Quietly tell your players to work more on skills and less on scoring

B. Get excited because some of the benchwarmers can get a little more playing time now

C. Cheer loudly every time your team scores and encourage your kid to keep doing super elaborate touchdown dances to celebrate CRUSHING the other team

How to score your quiz:

If you answered A or B for every single question, congratulations!! You are a badass sideline parent and I'll keep my fingers crossed that our rugrats end up on the same team even if your kid sucks at sports because I care less about winning and more about who I get to sit next to.

If you answered C for any of these questions, congratulations!! You get the title of A-hole F-wad D-bag sideline parent and kindly do not put your foldy chair anywhere near mine, otherwise I'll have to keep scooting over when you're not looking.

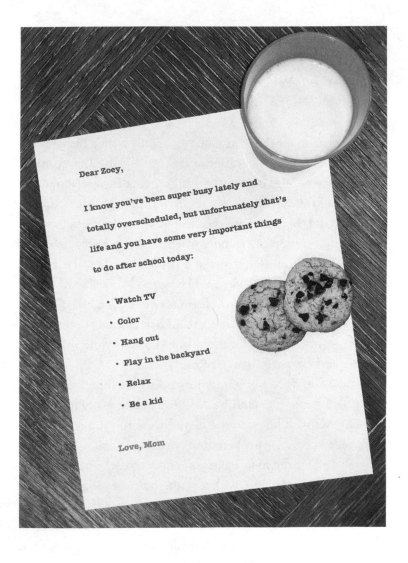

Dear Zoey,

I know you've been super busy lately and totally overscheduled, but unfortunately that's life and you have some very important things to do after school today:

- Watch TV
- Color
- Hang out
- Play in the backyard
- Relax
- Be a kid

Love, Mom

ONE LAST THING: IF IT ALL GOES ACCORDING TO PLAN, YOU'LL WALK AWAY WITH TWO THINGS: A WELL-ROUNDED KID AND HEMORRHOIDS

I know what you're thinking. That you really want a Hershey bar with a spoonful of peanut butter on top. Oh shit, never mind, that's what *I'm* thinking. You're thinking that I wrote about parents A LOT in a section about after-school activities. Damn straight I did. Because here's the thing: school activities are out of control. Sometimes I wonder whether things have just always been this way and now that I'm a parent I notice, but I don't think so. I mean, when I was a kid I was into ballet, like REALLY into it, and I took it ONE whole time a week. And I didn't really know any kids who took it more than that. It wasn't very serious. It was just fun. And at the end of the class everyone would line up and we'd each get a Tootsie Roll.

And I took soccer, too, and the games were super fun and no one yelled at me for standing on the field and just chewing my ribbons. Want to know why I played? Not to get a scholarship to college or because my parents were living vicariously through me. I played for the soda. I shit you not. At the end of each game a parent would show up with a giant cooler of soda cans and I would always take grape soda or orange soda and it was freezing cold and deeelicious. That is literally the reason I played soccer.

But today the parents are all freaking out about getting their kids into activities and driving to tournaments 100 miles away and yelling at the ref from the sidelines and jockeying to get their kids on certain teams, etc. etc. etc. So yeah, I think all this craziness is driven by the parents. So here's what we need to do. We just need to stop feeding the beast. We need to calmly sign our kids up for one or two activities a week and then sit on our little foldy chair or hard bench and watch until we get hemorrhoids. That's right, keep our mouths shut and just spectate (shit, I honestly thought spectate was a word but spell-check says it isn't). And believe me, I'm NOT one to speak. I've never yelled at a ref or a coach but there was one game this year where I "encouraged" Holden too much from the sidelines and he scolded me after the game and I wanted to crawl into a hole and shrivel up, I felt so bad. I've never done it again and I never will. I'm just gonna watch calmly and silently from now on.

Because here's the thing. While we're watching them, they're watching us. Yup, our kids can see the way we're behaving and we're setting an example. And when that father is yelling his head off and the ref comes over and tells him to GTFO and all the other parents are like, "Thank God," I know one person who's not like, "Good riddance." His kid. Somewhere on that field is a little boy or girl who just saw their dad get kicked out. And that's just sad. And you pretty much know that kid's gonna grow up to either A) need a lot of therapy or B) need a lot of anger management classes.

So we all just need to calm the F down. They're just after-school activities. And they're supposed to be fun. And they're supposed to teach our kids how to work hard, feel accomplished, feel defeated, feel creative, win nicely, lose nicely, work harder when you're losing, wear whatever color you're assigned, own the stage when you're the lead, yield the stage when you're not, try something new, discover a passion, and most of all understand that your parents are just there to watch you and cheer you on. Sometimes out loud and sometimes just in our heads.

———o———

The Hardest Thing about Being a Parent

IF YOU THINK ABOUT IT, the hardest thing about having kids isn't pushing a watermelon out of a hole that's the size of a base-ball, or helping them deal with a bully who keeps coming back like acid reflux, or learning math all over again to help them with their homework. It's the moment you realize they're gonna grow up. Yup, these little people who are constantly by your side and who your world revolves around are eventually going to walk out the door. Boohoohoo, noooooo!!!

One day you're praying they'll stop waking you up in the middle of the night and the next day you're crawling into their bed at 2 am because you miss them and they'll only cuddle with you when they're unconscious. It's crazy: You celebrate all of their milestones when they're babies — walking, talking, getting their first tooth — and then all of a sudden they've lost eight baby teeth and you're like "Stop losing body parts!!!" But there are a couple of things you can do to help. You can push down on their heads as much as possible and stop them from growing bigger (FYI, I'm still waiting to see if this one works), or you can stock up on a crapload of tissues and vodka for the day they leave you, or you can **_TRY_** (underlined, italicized, capitalized, and bolded on purpose) to embrace that they are growing up and attempt to help them get through it. Because the inevitable is inevitable, and eventually they're going to walk out the door.

The good news is, they always come back. If you do a good job, they'll come back because they want to. And if you F'ed up a lot, they'll come back because they need to. But either way, they'll come back. And if you followed everything I taught you in this book, they won't be a-holes.*

*Not a guarantee because like all parents, I don't really know WTF I'm doing.

No, this can't be happening. He's my baby!! No, no, noooooooooooooooooooo!!!!!!!!!!!! Don't leave me!!!!!! Stay, Holden, stayyyyy!!!!!!

- - - - - - - - -

TWELVE THINGS YOU SHOULD TRY TO TEACH YOUR DAUGHTER BEFORE SHE'S A WOMAN

1. To like her body. So she doesn't waste too much time wishing she had bigger boobs or smaller thighs or someone else's hair.
2. To be able to say no. Whether it's to a drunken frat guy, a cigarette, her scumbag boss, or just a friend who's trying to persuade her to lead the Girl Scout troop.
3. To treat anxiety or depression the same way she'd treat strep throat. Like a common illness she shouldn't be ashamed of, but something she needs to get help for.
4. To be able to leave the house without makeup. To be able to do her makeup so it looks like she's not wearing any. And above all else, to know that she's beautiful no matter how much (or how little) makeup she's wearing.
5. To ask for a raise when she deserves it, and to ask for more than she deserves so there's room for negotiations AND just in case she's undervaluing herself.
6. To brag more about the things she gets for a bargain than the things she spends a lot on. Anyone with money can go out and buy a Tesla, but it takes real skill to be able to comb the racks at HomeGoods and find a painting that looks like it came from a fancy gallery.
7. To get married because she wants to, not because she needs to.

8. To always have a bank account of her own, to put half the bills in her name, and to know how most shit works around the house. No one ever plans on getting divorced or widowed, so everyone needs to be prepared for it.

9. To know that she can easily change what a person wears or eats or how much they floss, but that if they ever lay a hand on her, there's no changing that. Just walk away. On second thought, run.

10. To remember that everything seems worse at 2 am. Try to go back to sleep and confront it in the morning.

11. To know that being able to produce a baby isn't what will make her a successful woman. Some of the most incredible women on earth adopt. And some don't have children at all.

12. To treat other women like gold. The world makes it hard enough on women already that we don't need to make it even harder on each other.

ME: Who knows, Zoey, YOU could be the first female president one day!

ZOEY: Uggh, I hope not.

ME: You don't want to be president?

ZOEY: I just don't want to be the *first* one. That's too long to wait for a girl president.

WHEN IT'S TIME TO TURN PUBLIC DISPLAYS OF AFFECTION INTO PRIVATE DISPLAYS OF AFFECTION

Dear Zoey,

This morning I pulled up to your school to drop you and a friend off and you did something. Something you've never done before. When I said, "Give me a kiss," you giggled and said, "Mommmm, no." It wasn't in a mean way. I could tell you were just embarrassed in front of your friend. And you must have noticed the mega depressed look on my face because you kissed me anyway.

But guess what? I get it. I was a kid once too, you know. Back when cell phones and the Internet didn't exist yet and dinosaurs stomped the earth, I remember feeling that way.

Last year when you were still little, I used to say that I would never let you leave the car without kissing me. If you tried, I would yell out the window, "I LOVE YOU, ZOEEEYYYYY!!!!" and embarrass you even more, ensuring that the next day you would make sure to stop and kiss me before you walked away. But I'm not going to do that anymore.

I'd like to make a deal with you. Here are the terms. You don't have to kiss me when you're leaving my car every morning. Nope, that whole sentence is not a typo. I actually just said that. From now on you can just give me a smile and a wave and say, "Bye, Mom!" and I'll do the same. On ONE condition. You are legally required to kiss me once before we walk out of the house. I don't care if I'm screaming at you to get your shoes on. I don't care if you're having a gigantic fight with your brother. I don't care if we're like 9,000 minutes late. We will stop and give each other a little hug and kiss before we get in the car.

Because as much as you need to maintain your dignity on the elementary school playground, I need my kiss every morning. I need it more than breakfast, more than coffee, more than anything. That one little kiss gets me through the day.

Deal?

Love,
Mom

ZOEY: Mom, what are thongs?
ME: Ummm, thongs, hmmmm, they're kind of like underwear but skinny in the back so they kind of go into your butt. Where did you hear about them?
ZOEY: In my magazine, see? It says, "Which do you wear, thongs or flip-flops?"

Today Holden said my legs are fat. And I'm so glad he did. I mean, don't get me wrong, at first it stung. But then I thought about it. When I was in the fifth or sixth grade, my class went on a field trip and while we were on the bus, the boys "designed" their perfect girl. They were like, let's use Lucy's hair, and Claudia's eyes, and should we use Alyssa's legs or Katie's, and then they would debate which were better, and they meticulously picked through the girls in our class to create this fantasy girl. And if the other girls on that bus were anything like me, they were listening closely. Listening to hear if the boys would pick them for anything. Or how they would critique their body parts. At some point the boys agreed to use my lips. That was 35 years ago and I still remember it. But there were girls who weren't picked. There were girls who had to listen to them say, nope, not hers. There were girls who had to hear them say things like, "No way, too many freckles" or "Her belly is fat." I'm sure there are plenty of girls from my grade who still have memories burned in their brain just like me from that day. So I'm glad Holden told me my legs are fat. It gave me a chance to talk to him now and teach him how that can really hurt a girl's feelings. I'm 47, and I can take it. So I'm so glad he said it to me so that hopefully he'll never say it to a girl his age, a girl who won't be able to shrug it off the way I can.

BOYS WILL NOT BE BOYS

Can we just talk about the phrase "Boys will be boys" for a sec? It exists for one reason only — to excuse bad behavior. Like if you saw a boy help an old lady cross the street, you would never say, "Boys will be boys." Nope, you're more likely to say it after a boy punches someone at recess, or when boys are having a burping contest, or when a guy takes a raunchy photo holding his hands over his coworker's boobs while she's sleeping. Basically, the phrase could be changed to "Boys will be violent," or "Boys will be gropers," or "Boys will be a-holes unless we teach them not to do this kind of shit anymore." Because one of the reasons boys will be boys is because we let them get away with it.

So let's start teaching our boys how to behave from a young age, how to respect their moms and their sisters and the girls in their grade. So boys won't be boys. They'll be gentlemen. Here goes: ten things to teach our boys if we want them to respect women:

1. Always call a woman Miss, Mrs., Ms., ma'am, or just by her name. Not babe, ho, chick, honey, sweetie, or some other word that sounds casual even though it's derogatory. You

might think it sounds cool but guess who doesn't? Fifty
percent of the population.

2. Judge a girl by her brain. We know the first thing you might
notice is her face or her legs or her boobs. That's okay. You
can't see her brain until you get to know her. So that's what
you'll have to do.

3. If you work under an intelligent woman, respect her. If you
work over an intelligent woman, promote her.

4. If a girl gets her period and you happen to see, don't say
"eww" or "gross" or whisper to your friend. The only thing
you should whisper is, "Would you like to borrow my
sweatshirt to tie around your waist?"

5. If a woman is walking behind you, open the door for
her. Whether it's your girlfriend, a complete stranger, or
someone who'll get into the Starbucks line ahead of you.
Getting your coffee thirty seconds later isn't that big a deal,
but being a d-bag is.

6. No means no. Period. Yes, women can be a little confusing
sometimes, like when we ask you which shoes look better
and you tell us and we say thanks but go with the other
ones. But when we say "no," there's nothing confusing about
it. And if we're too drunk to say "no," just assume we're
saying it.

7. If a woman is nice enough to say "yes," don't brag about it
the next day. The men's locker room is full of dicks. Don't
be one of them.

8. If you want to break up with a girl, just do it. It's better to
break up with someone nicely than to act crappy until she
has to do it herself.

9. You have a mom. You might have a sister. You might have a daughter one day. Treat every woman you come across the way you would want them to be treated.

10. Remember where you came from. A vagina. Respect it.

- - - - - - - - -

Boys will be boys.

- - - - - - - - -

ZOEY: Dad, what does the F-word mean?

HUBBY: Uhhhh, you're only nine. I don't know if you're supposed to know that.

ZOEY: Dad, I'm old enough. What does it mean?

HUBBY: It means (quietly whispers) fuck.

ZOEY: Daaaad, I know THAT!! Like shit means poop, but what does fuck mean?

HUBBY: Ohhh, it means to have sex.

And right when it came out of his mouth, he knew. Awww shit, he shouldn't have said that.

ZOEY: (thinking) To have sex? What, like gender?

And he should have explained what sex is right then and there but he was not prepared.

HUBBY: Ummm, yeah. Like gender.

So if Zoey asks what fuck you are, please just say male or female. At least until I sit down with her and straighten out this mess.

STOP CALLING IT A VAJAYJAY
(AND OTHER THINGS TO DO WHEN
YOU HAVE THE SEX TALK)

Awwwww shit, it's time to have THAT conversation. Yup, the birds and the bees. How babies are made. But I know what you're thinking. How do you know it's time? (translation: Do I *have to* yet?) Okay, so basically you know it's time to have THE conversation one of two ways. 1. Your kiddo asks how babies are made, or 2. Your kiddo is at risk of finding out from someone else. Sorry, I know this is like the last thing you want to do right now (or ever), but it's time to stop beating around the bush and talk about the bush. And what goes in it. But don't you worry, you're not in this alone. I've pulled together this handy list of tips that'll help you get through this difficult time in your life. So here goes. Twelve things to keep in mind when you think it might be time to talk to your douchenugget about s-e-x.

1. Teach them before someone else does
Picture this. Adorable little Sarabeth is playing hopscotch at recess when all of a sudden little Thor comes up to her and starts chanting, "The penis goes in the vagina, the penis goes in the vagina!!" And poor little Sarabeth is sitting there like WHAAAAAT? And now she's scarred for life and wants to run off and join a convent. Which doesn't sound all that bad, except how are you gonna score yourself some grandbabies if Sarabeth refuses to ever do the nasty (insert heebie-jeebies emoji here)?

2. Don't just let your kids find
out about sex in sex ed

I mean, yeah, I'm sure there are plenty of parents who do this but I'm kinda of the mindset that you don't want to learn for the first time that a penis goes into a vagina in front of the boy you have a crush on.

3. Don't just assume your kiddo is
gonna ask you how babies are made

Some kids ask why the sky is blue, some kids ask why your boobs hang low, and some kids ask what a condom is so you tell them allllll about what a condom is and about nine-tenths of the way through your explanation you realize they meant a condiment. But seriously, your kid might never ask how babies are made, so you gotta figure out a way to broach the subject. "Speaking of hot dogs, Little Timmy . . ."

4. Pick a private place to have the talk

Don't go to a crowded restaurant where you're sitting two inches from a couple who's out on their first date. Your kid's gonna be like, "Wait, does that guy put his penis in her vagina?!" And in order to get the answer, you have to lean over and ask, "Hey, did you guys meet on eHarmony or Tinder?"

5. Have visual aids

No, not like porn. I mean have an age-appropriate illustrated book to open up in case they need visuals to understand or to leave in their bedroom in case you can't get through the conversation.

6. Use real anatomical words

The following words are off-limits: bagina, vajayjay, hoo-ha, coochie, wienie, noodle, tallywhacker, wee wee, cookie, front butt, and pretty much any other word your doctor would never use. The words are penis and vagina. And you've gotta say them without laughing. No one said this was gonna be easy, people.

7. Don't offer too much information

So here's the thing. You're just giving them the bare-bones explanation of how a baby is made. You're not talking about foreplay or BJs or positions or sex toys or anything else. I know it's gonna seem like a short conversation. That's a GOOD thing, people.

8. Make sure to remind them that it only happens when you're a grownup who's in love

And try not to mention that time you drank too many strawberry daiquiris at The Zoo Bar in college and did it with uhhhh, hmmmm, what was his name again?

9. Don't talk about how fun it is

This is a conversation about making babies. NOT about doing the horizontal mambo.

10. Be prepared and UNprepared for questions

If they ask you something and you don't know the answer, say, "Hmm, lemme think before I answer and scar you for life."

11. Make them solemnly swear NOT to tell anyone else what they just learned

Or before you know it, little Sarabeth's parents are going to be sending you the tuition bill for the convent.

12. Make them solemnly, SOLEMNLY swear that they will never EVER look any of this up on the Internet

Or your kid's gonna start singing bow chicka bow bow every time the doorbell rings and it's the pizza delivery guy.

- - - - - - - - -

TIP: When you want to talk to your kid about something that might be a little embarrassing, do it in the car so you don't have to look at each other. And have them sit on the passenger side so you don't accidentally make eye contact in the rearview mirror.

- - - - - - - - -

WELL HOLY CRAP, I GUESS THERE IS ONE GOOD REASON TO OWN A GUINEA PIG

ZOEY: Mommm, we need to trim the guinea pig's nails!!
ME: Whatta you mean we have to cut his nails?
ZOEY: They're too long. We have to cut them.

WTF?

I mean, no, I don't say WTF out loud because my daughter is only nine and I attempt not to curse in front of her (it's not my fault if I accidentally think words out loud sometimes). But I mean, come on people, I'm not running a nail salon for rodents here. And they did NOT tell us we would have to trim his nails back in the pet store when we bought him, along with 9 million other things they failed to tell us (like the fact that this animal must have nine butts and constantly eat Ex-Lax). Seriously, picture a cage that is literally floor to ceiling with poop because that's what we're talking about. Anyways, I peek into the cage at Hey-Hey-Twix (she changed his name so I just call him both now), and yup, his nails are like four inches long. Picture Flo-Jo with fur.

ME: Fine, bring him to the bathroom.

At which point Zoey goes to get him out of the cage.

ZOEY: Mommm, HELPPPPP, I can't get him!!!!!

I'm tempted to yell at her to stop yelling, but I've already yelled at her like 9,000 times in the past ten minutes, so I decide to be nice and try to help. I drop down to the ground and reach into the cage. I try to grab him, he runs under his dome. I lift up the dome, he runs into his tube. I tilt the tube and his scary little Edward Scissorhands cling to the edge of the tube so he won't fall out so I gently start tapping the tube to knock his finger-nails loose, but it doesn't work so I start banging the tube a lit-tle harder until Zoey starts screaming that I'm hurting him, and since I'm not Jeffrey Dahmer, I stop torturing small animals and put the tube down. At which point the rodent casually walks out, gives me the middle finger, and walks straight into Zoey's hands.

ZOEY: Awwwww, come here, sweetie pie. (paraphrased)
Was that big mean mommy abusing you?

She starts rubbing him and cooing to him and trying to calm him down, making me feel like a complete a-hole for scaring him to death (I wish literally). And then we go into the bathroom to clip his nails.

This could get messy, so I make Zoey cradle the little furball in a blanket. Okay, remember when you had a toddler and you had to cut their nails and it was pretty much impossible? That. Was. Nothing. Cutting a guinea pig's nails is like defusing a bomb that's inside that thing that shakes the paint cans at Home Depot.

After about 9,000 tries (slight exaggeration, more like 8,000) I finally manage to clip off the tiniest millimeter of one of his Flo-Jo fingernails. Awesome, only 15¾ to go. So I go for the next nail but this time I have the complete opposite problem. I go to clip his nail and the guy flinches and I end up cutting wayyyyy too close.

GUINEA PIG: Reeeeekk, reeeeeeekk, reeeeeeek!!!!

Oh, what, you don't speak guinea pig? Fine.

TRANSLATION: What the F you motherF'er you cut
    my finger!!!!!
ZOEY: Mommmmmmm!!!!!!!!!

And I'm screaming sorry and Zoey's screaming bloody murder and the guinea pig is freaking out and jumps out of her lap and starts running around on the floor leaving little dots of blood behind him with his extra long toenails click click click clicking everywhere. While the whole time, there are three words going through my head over and over again. F.U. PetSmart. F.U. PetSmart. F.U. PetSmart. But I digress.

Anyways, Zoey finally manages to catch him again and cuddle him in the blanket while she sits on the toilet with big fat tears rolling down her cheeks.

ZOEY: I can't do this!!

ME: Yes you can.

ZOEY: No I can't! Can't we just take him to PetSmart to cut them?

ME: Zoey, if this guinea pig ever steps foot in PetSmart again, he's staying there.

Wait, can we do that? Like can I bring him back to PetSmart and return him? What would I say to them?

ME: Ummm, I think this guinea pig is broken because poop just keeps falling out of the back of him.

But Zoey starts bawling louder when I say this, so I know what I have to do.

ME: Zoey, we are going to do this.

ZOEY: Noooo, Mom, I can't!!!

ME: Yes you can.

ZOEY: I CAN'T!!!!

ME: YES. YOU. CANNNN.

And that's when I bend down to get eye level with her and I use my most serious "I mean business" voice.

ME: Zoey Lila Alpert, you listen to me. You are his mommy, and that means you have to take care of him. It's *your* job, even when it gets hard. Mommies do not give up, do you understand me?

ZOEY: Yes.

And we do it. It takes a lonnnng time, and it sucks a lot, and I'm pretty sure all the stress will shorten that guinea pig's life by a couple of years (hopefully), and probably mine too (definitely), but we do it. I accomplish something I didn't want to do, and she accomplishes something she didn't think she could do. And she gets a very important lesson about what it'll be like to be a mother one day. To a real baby, not just a furry poop machine.

Sometimes when I remember she's gonna move out one day, I realize how important it is to spend as much time as possible together.

ME: Night night, Zoey.

- - - - - - - - -

AWWWW SHIT,
THEY WERE RIGHT.
BIGGER KIDS,
BIGGER PROBLEMS

Little problem: Your toddler Super-Glued himself to the cereal aisle floor because you won't buy him Sugary Boogery O's.

Solution: Stand your ground.

Big problem: You just discovered your kid is chatting online with a possible pedophile.

Solution: Grab your cell phone, head to the bathroom where you can shit bricks and call the police at the same time.

Little problem: Your three-year-old just asked loudly in the public restroom why you pulled a red mouse out of your bagina.

Solution: Tell him you'll explain later and then forget to explain later unless he asks again.

Big problem: Your daughter just found out she's not invited to a giant sleepover party and she's devastated.

Solution: Have a special movie night for the two of you and make it as awesome as possible but still know it won't make up for the sleepover party she's missing.

Little problem: Your four-year-old's butt has been itching at night and you go spelunking with a flashlight and find pinworms.

Solution: Get the medicine to fix it.

Big problem: When you ask your son what he learned in school today, he says he learned a new word — the "N" word.

Solution: Take deep breaths and try to remain calm while you explain to him how awful that word is . . . and that you'll kill him if he ever uses it.

Little problem: You just asked your son a question while he was peeing and he turned to answer and spray-painted the entire bathroom in urine.

Solution: Never do that again.

Big problem: Your kid isn't ready for a cell phone but the rest of his friends have cell phones so you can either be the BAD mommy who caves and gives him one or the MEAN mommy who doesn't.

Solution: No F'ing idea, sometimes there isn't one.

HOLDEN: Mom, how does the baby come out of
the fagina?

ME: Wait, what did you call it?

HOLDEN: The fagina.

ME: Va, VA, with a "v."

HOLDEN: Okay, but how does it come out?

ME: Well, when a mommy is having a baby, the VAgina gets
a little bigger so the baby can come out.

HOLDEN: How does it know to do that?

ME: The body has been growing that baby for nine months,
so it knows when it's time.

HOLDEN: That's gross.

ME: No, it's not gross at all. It's beautiful. That's where ALL
babies come from.

HOLDEN: I didn't.

ME: Well, that's true. Sometimes if something goes wrong,
they have to take the baby out of the mommy's tummy.
But almost all babies do. Your friends all came out of
their mommies' vaginas.

HOLDEN: No.

ME: Yes. Carlos, Andrew, Antony, Elliott, Luke.

HOLDEN: Not Luke.

ME: Yes, Luke.

HOLDEN: Mom, there is NO way Luke came out of
a vagina.

ME: Of course he did.

HOLDEN: I'm sure he did NOT. Luke would NOT
do that.

ME: Well, we can ask his mom.
HOLDEN: Now. Ask her.
ME: Ummmm.

But I decide it's important to teach Holden that even the "coolest" of his friends came out of vaginas, so I type up the weirdest text I've ever sent.

TEXT: Very crazy question for you. Did you have a
    C-section for Luke?

It seemed too weird to ask if Luke came out of her vagina. And I immediately see the dots that she's typing back.

TEXT BACK: Actually I did have C-sections. For
    both babies!

Oh crap.

HOLDEN: What did she say?
ME: You were right. But all your other friends came out of
    their mommies' vaginas.
HOLDEN: See? I knew Luke wouldn't do that.

- - - - - - - - -

AN HONEST
LETTER TO GIRLS

To the Girls,

I'm sorry, we've lied to you. The truth is we've been lying to you all these years. You know how we've always been like rah rah sis boom bah, girl power, being a girl is awesome, yada yada yada, girls rule!! Well, that's bullshit. Being a girl is not all that and a bag of chips. Sometimes it downright sucks.

Like when you have a brand-new baby and your boss doesn't give you some plum assignment because he just assumes you already have too much on your plate. Or when you have to spend a bazillion hours looking for a dress because you already wore the dress you own like six times, but your boyfriend can wear the same suit he's been wearing since his bar mitzvah 25 years ago. Or when you're out on a hike and the guys can just whip it out and pee on any tree and you have to figure out how the hell to crouch down and find the perfect trajectory so the pee doesn't cling to your thigh and split into two streams and spray all over your pants. Or when you say exactly the same thing as your coworker and everyone thinks you're a bitch for saying it but they think he's a leader. Yup, it sucks. And like a million other things too.

I mean, yeah, we could keep lying to you and say that being a girl is awesome, but that's pretty much the crappiest thing we can do because our job is to prepare you for the real world, not some fantasy world where women are treated equally and fly on unicorns that poop rainbows.

But (I hope you knew there was a *but* coming) BUT you can whine and cry and say "no fair," OR you can say "F that shit." The reason they call it the glass ceiling is because no one can see it. Yup, it's invisible. Which means you don't need to see it either. Ignore that clear sheet of glass and climb that ladder and keep on climbing, and if your head hits something hard, put on a helmet and ram the shit out of it until it shatters. And if someone at work thinks you're a bitch for being assertive, you just assert yourself and say something like, "Does it make you uncomfortable when I take on a leadership role?" and see what they do the next time you're assertive. And if someone says you throw like a girl, you tell him, "That's funny because you think like a douche." And if your boss doesn't give you the plum assignment because you have too much "mommy stuff" on your plate and he hands it to some dad who supposedly has less at home to deal with (cough cough bullshit), you march into your boss's office and say, "Listen, do you know the reason God gave women the ability to give birth? Because we can handle shit. Please remember that the next time you're handing out assignments." And if you're hiking with a bunch of guys and you have to pee, well, sorry, there's not much you can do about that one. But hey, men can't give birth through their penises (penae?), so no, we can't pee on trees but maybe our equipment actually is superior.

So there you go. The truth. You can handle it, and sooooo much more. Wanna know why? Because you're a girl.

Honestly yours,
The Women

- - - - - - - - - -

WAIT, HORMONES AT NINE, ARE YOU KIDDING ME?!!!

WTH is going on? Yesterday I had this sweet little innocent love muffin (if you ignore the tantrums and the refusals to go to bed and the writing on the wall, as in literally her name written on the wall in a big fat Sharpie, but she was mostly this innocent happy little girl), and today I have this totally hormonal tween-ager who might explode if I breathe!! Not if I breathe too loud. I mean, if I breathe AT ALL.

WTF?! She's NOT a teenager yet. She's nine!! Back in my day, kids didn't hit puberty until they were at least 27 (slight exaggeration ... unless they were gymnasts). But these days, NINE. I blame it all on hand sanitizer and hormones and pesticides and 409. Just kidding. I'm not a brilliant scientist so I have no F'ing idea why kids are "blossoming" earlier these days. But they are. And even though it sucks ass for everyone, luckily my daughter is on the younger side in her grade so I was warned in advance before these raging hormones hit. So I was ready. Bwahahahaha, not.

There is literally NO WAY to be ready for what's coming. Like you know those movies when someone knows aliens are invading the planet so they're stupidly crouched in the closet ready to defend themselves with a frying pan? That's basically what I was like before the hormones showed up. Only it wasn't a frying pan. It was a shoebox of chocolate and a bottle of vodka. And technically I was already in my closet with those things long before she hit nine, but I doubled the supply before she became a tween.

And there I was sitting with my mouth wrapped around a Hershey bar and a bottle of Grey Goose (total lie, I buy the Costco brand) while I waited. And waited. And waited. And then one day, I pick her up from school to go to the ice rink and holy crap, heeeere we go.

ME: Hey, Zoey.
ZOEY: (itty-bitty mouse voice) Hi, Mommy.
ME: Are you crying? What's wrong?
ZOEY: Everything.

Did you just hear that cracking noise? That, my friends, is the sound of my heart breaking.

ME: Did something happen at school?
ZOEY: No.
ME: Did you have a fight with someone?

ZOEY: No.

ME: Did you get hurt in P.E.?

ZOEY: No. I just felt sad all day. Like I couldn't stop crying.

OMG what's wrong with her? Is she depressed? Is she going to start wearing black? Will she get her ears pierced with those big hoop thingies that stretch out your earlobes so they dangle like those women on the cover of *National Geographic* and the baristas at Starbucks? Why is she sad? She has the most perfect life ever. People don't just randomly feel sad for no reason. Well, once a month I do, but that's just—awwwww crap, and that's when I realize what's going on. Hormones. It's official. She's a tween.

ME: Oh, honey, I think you're feeling hormones. It's totally normal at your age. Let's just go to ice skating practice.

ZOEY: (teary-eyed) Mom, I don't want to ice skate anymore. I want to quit.

ME: Whatta you mean?! You *love* ice skating.

ZOEY: I hate it.

ME: Well, we've already paid for today, so let's go and then we can talk about everything after.

Seriously, this is me all the time. My kids might be dying of Ebola but if we have tickets to Great America I'll be like, "Well, we already paid for it so let's go. You can die later after we ride roller coasters."

Anyways, Zoey goes out on the ice while I sit in the stands having images of worst-case scenarios of things she might do when the hormones are raging in junior high school. Cutting herself, battling bulimia, committing suicide, listening to Celine Dion on volume 10. And just as I'm imagining all of these horrible possibilities, I look out at the ice and I see my girl. Smiling. Laughing. Spinning. Yayyyy, she's all better!!! So on our way home, I say something to her.

ME: You feeling a little better?

ZOEY: A little.

ME: You were just having a moment.

ZOEY: Whatta you mean, a moment?

ME: Ummm, how do I explain this? It's like a feeling that comes over you for a moment.

ZOEY: But it wasn't a moment. It was a whole day.

ME: Yeah, that's the thing about moments. Sometimes they last longer than a moment. The important thing to remember is that you don't want to make any BIG decisions while you're having a moment.

ZOEY: Like what?

And my head thinks of lots of bad things, but luckily I think of a more appropriate one to say to her.

ME: Like quitting ice skating.

ZOEY: (Gasp) I would NEVER quit ice skating!! I *need* to ice skate. It's like air.

ME: Okayyy. But remember like an hour ago on the way to the rink you were saying you want to quit? Aren't you glad you didn't?

ZOEY: Phew, that would have been *really* bad.
ME: Right. See? No big decisions while you're having
a moment.
ZOEY: Got it.

As much as I hate that she's turning into a tween now, I'm kind of thankful for it.

When I was a kid you went straight from being a kid to being a teenager. There was no middle ground. Now they've added a level in between. I don't know who the F "they" is, but someone did. And thank God. The tween years are when the hormones start kicking in and it's a small glimpse into the years that are coming up. And it gives us a little warning and time to start teaching our kiddos how to deal with the shit in small doses before they actually run into the shit full throttle. And as parents, the tween years give us time to adjust and make us feel like we're a little prepared. Even though we're not prepared at all. We're screwed. Very, very screwed.

It happened when Holden was about five. I was putting him to bed and closing his door when he said . . .

HOLDEN: I love you more than you love me.

It was adorable but there was no F'ing way he loves me more than I love him.

ME: Not possible. Good night, buddy.

And the next night it happened again.

HOLDEN: I love you more than you love me.
ME: Not possible.

And the next night it happened again, and the next, and the next, and the next. And each time I said "not possible." So then one night he changed it.

HOLDEN: I love you more than you love me yes possible.

So then I started trying to say "not possible" really quickly to beat him to the punch. So he started saying it faster.

HOLDEN: Iloveyoumorethanyoulovemeyespossible.
ME: NOT possible.
HOLDEN: But I said it first.

So then it became a race to see who could say it first every time.

HOLDEN:
IloveyoumorethanyoulovemeyespossibleIsaiditfirst.

So now this is what he says every night when I shut the door. I love you more than you love me yes possible I said it first. And even though it's a total lie and there's no way he loves me more than I love him, I hope he keeps saying it like this forever.

ONE LAST THING:
A LETTER TO
MY DOUCHENUGGETS

Dear future NON a-holes (hopefully!!!!),

Yeah, I know I've been writing this whole book to parents, but I'm writing this last chapter to you. I want you to picture something. Close your eyes. Shit, no wait, don't close your eyes because then you can't read. Oh crap, are you sitting there with your eyes closed already and wondering when you're supposed to open them again? I'm telepathically sending you a message right now. "Open your eyes!"

Okay, now keep your eyes open but picture this in your head. Picture a path that's littered with allllll kinds of crap — cigarettes, guns, needles, bullies, bad grades, bad guys, poisonous shrooms, fun shrooms, meth, meanies, laziness (I don't know WTF that looks like but maybe sloths or something), junk food, dirty clothes, trash, etc. etc. etc. Okay, do you have that picture in your head? All righty then.

You know what would be so easy for me to do? If I just took a big motherF'ing broom and swept that whole path clean so you could march on down that empty road easy peasy. I can totally do that. You'd never screw up, you'd never get hurt, and God forbid you tripped on the empty sidewalk (heyyy, who put that sidewalk there?!), it wouldn't be a big deal. Because I'd be there to pick you up, brush you off, kiss your boo-boo, and put a Band-

Aid on it, even if it's not bleeding and doesn't really need one. Heck, I could even carry you down that path if that's what you want.

Or . . .

I could leave that path how it is. That's right, leave allllllll that scary, dangerous, mean, boo-boo-making, cancer-causing, deadly shit right there in front of you. And I could teach you how to navigate that path yourself. How to step over the weapons, brush aside the drugs, walk around the dangers, pick yourself up, pick the trash up, say hi to the bad people but keep walking past them, dry your own tears, etc. etc. etc.

Because that path goes on for millions of miles and years and years and one day I might not be there with my big F'ing broom to sweep it clean for you. Maybe I'll be in a different house, or a different state, or just upstairs in the bathroom pooping. And then what? If I taught you how to deal with all that scary shit on your own, you can keep on walking and navigate it without me and you'll be okay. But if I've been there the whole time making it easy/safe/hunky-dory for you, well then, how are you going to do it when I'm gone?

So I know you think I'm being mean sometimes when you ask for a fork and I'm standing right next to the silverware drawer and I'm like get it yourself and you're like but you're closer to the silverware drawer and I'm like don't be lazy and just use the legs I gave you to get your own damn fork. Wow, that was a long sentence. Anyways, my point is this. I'm not trying to be mean or lazy. I mean, seriously, my life would be a helluva lot easier if I just grabbed the fork FOR you. But nope, I can't do that. I mean, I can and you'll quit whining and torturing my ears, but I WON'T do that.

Unless . . .

I'm giving you an option here. Unless you agree to never ever grow up. That's right, stay our cute little babies forever (personally speaking, around six years old would be a nice sweet spot but I'll accept anything up to ten) and I will always get that damn fork for you. Wait, why are you shaking your head no? What?! That doesn't sound good to you? I'll get you ALL the forks in the world and I'll keep making you lunches and bringing you snacks and figuring out why the remote isn't working and setting up playdates and schlepping you to fun activities and planning your birthday parties!! Doesn't that sound amazing?! And you can keep holding my hand and sitting on my lap and crawling into my bed and hugging me, even at awkward times like when I'm on the toilet. No? Sigh. Okay, fine.

Then there are gonna be times I'm not gonna get you the fork, and times I'll say no to screen time, and times I'll accidentally cut your brownie a millimeter smaller than your brother's and tell you to deal with it, and times I'll make you clean your room before you go outside, and times I won't let you wear a crop top to your aunt's birthday dinner that I'm making you go to instead of going to the mall with that douchebag a-hole you like. But one day when you're a totally happy kickass successful amazing adult who's conquering the world, I hope you'll understand why I did all those things. It's

because I didn't want you to become an a-hole. And
even though I probably did a million things wrong along
the way, clearly I did something right. Because ultimately
you turned out to be pretty F'ing awesome. And I am
SOOOO incredibly proud of you.

Love,
Your mom

P.S. I left your shit on the stairs, so please bring it to your
room today. Not tomorrow. And please don't make me
ask again. And are you trying to air-condition the whole
neighborhood? Close the door. And lock it. Do you
want a bad guy to get in and rob us and murder us in our
sleep? Is that what you want?

P.P.S. I love you.

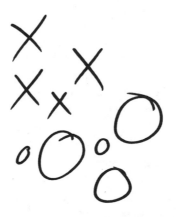

ACKNOWLEDGMENTS

Okay, would the following people please step forward to receive your giant, heartfelt, crotch-to-crotch hugs from me? None of those half-ass, sideways, only lean in with our top half hugs. Nope, you deserve my appreciation big time because there is no way I could have written this book without you.

Zoey and Holden, please step up first. You never cease to amaze me. You amazed me when you were little and projectile vomited so forcefully it hit a wall six feet away, and you amaze me now with your kindness, creativity, love for each other, and like a million other things.

My hubby, you're up next. Without you I would be nowhere. No, that's not true. I'd probably be at the bottom of a dark closet drinking something hard and eating chocolate. I mean more than I already do. Thank you so much for being my love, my sanity, and my partner in raising these two non a-holes.

Rachel Sussman, please step up to the plate. Thank you for being my guide every time I have the crazy notion to write a book. I think we need to add a slash to your name. It should now read agent/friend.

Deb Brody and Emma Peters, come on down for your full-body hugs. I think you have bodies. I mean, we've only met on Zoom (damn you, COVID-19) but I assume you are more than just torsos. In all seriousness, thank you and everyone at Houghton Mifflin Harcourt for helping me turn a very rough draft into something I can be proud of.

Neil Swaab, it's your turn now. Thank you for punctuating my words with your hilarious illustrations.

To all the moms out there who have read my books or the things I put on social media every day, a huge crotch-to-crotch hug to you too. This parenting gig may be the hardest job on earth, but your support makes it a little easier.

And last but not least, a huge thank you to my own parents for not letting their babies grow up to be a-holes. At least I think I'm not an a-hole. Usually.